A Study of the Strategy and Tactics
of the
SHENANDOAH VALLEY CAMPAIGN,
1861-1862.

A Study of the Strategy and Tactics

of the

SHENANDOAH VALLEY CAMPAIGN

1861-1862

WITH SIX MAPS

Illustrating the

PRINCIPLES OF WAR

BATTLES DESCRIBED.

BY

A. KEARSEY, D.S.O., O.B.E., p.s.c.

LATE LIEUTENANT-COLONEL GENERAL STAFF

The Naval & Military Press Ltd

Published by

The Naval & Military Press Ltd

Unit 5 Riverside, Brambleside
Bellbrook Industrial Estate
Uckfield, East Sussex
TN22 1QQ England

Tel: +44 (0)1825 749494

www.naval–military-press.com
www.nmarchive.com

CONTENTS

MAPS.

The Shenandoah Valley:
   First Bull Run, 21st July, '61.
   Kernstown, 23rd March, '62.
   McDowell, 8th May, '62.
   Winchester, 25th May, '62.
   Cross Keys, 8th June, '62.
   Port Republic, 9th June, '62.

SHENANDOAH VALLEY CAMPAIGN, 1861-1862

CHAPTER I.

GENERAL SUMMARY.

THIS Campaign is particularly interesting at the present time. To-day there are many arguments brought forward for the relaxation of national expenditure in insurance by the reduction of our navy, army, and air force. Insurance is a necessity, not an extravagance. As human nature is what is it, war can never become an impossibility.

REASONS FOR THE WAR.

In a country among a people speaking the same language because there were conflicting interests, there was war for four years as recently as 1865. On either side relations fought because they disagreed. In some of the southern states of America the inhabitants considered that it was necessary to employ slaves on their tobacco, cotton, and sugar estates.

The Republicans used machinery for the production of their manufactures and looked on slavery as dispensable. In the South the representatives of the States considered that they could secede from the union if they disagreed with the Central Government's policy.

The rulers of the North would not alter their views. Thus eleven Confederate States and twenty-two Federal States fought one another from April 13th, 1861, till April 9th, 1865. The fighting on both sides was very fierce. At the battle of Sharpsburg, for instance, in six hours there were 13,000 casualties.

To-day, with the numerous nations in Europe controlled by democratic, and, consequently, sensitive governments, there are more points of friction than there could have been in one country in 1861. The moral is that a nation must be always prepared for war.

PLANS OF CAMPAIGN.

Owing to the sudden creation of the Confederate States, Richmond, the capital, became an important point for the Federals to capture. If the seat of the Confederate Government was captured the loss of prestige to the Confederate cause would be of the greatest influence in the struggle.

Therefore the Federals considered that though other operations were important, the most weighty were those directed towards the Confederate capital. In addition, Virginia became the main theatre of war, because in it was the Confederate main field army, which, if not defeated, was a constant menace to Washington. The moral effect of the capture of the Federal capital would have been considerable, and the practical effect would have been the secession from the Union of Maryland and Delaware. Also a decisive victory for the South would probably have caused it to be recognized as a belligerent power by some of the countries in Europe.

Therefore, as to either side, it was important to capture the other seat of Government, the country lying between Washington and Richmond would form the theatre of important operations. The Federal plan, then, was to seize their enemy's chief city and centre of rebellion, and also to destroy the field army protecting it. The Federal campaign was conducted on double and exterior lines; that of their opponents was on single and interior lines.

Before the opening of the campaign in 1862, the courses open to McClellan were : —

(1) To advance directly against the Confederate main army.

(2) To turn their right flank and to reach Richmond without directly crushing the Confederate army.

(3) To turn their left flank advancing by the Shenandoah Valley, or by the eastern slopes of the Blue Ridge Mountains. In this case the distance for his turning movement was too great, and the line of communications would have been dangerously liable to interruption when the army turned in an easterly direction towards Richmond.

Nor could the Federals have moved their large forces along the few available roads without the aid of the railway. Their line of communications below Gordonsville would be exposed to a flank attack. Actually McClellan carried out the second plan by moving his troops by sea to the Yorktown Peninsula between the York and James Rivers. It was also necessary to leave a sufficient force to ensure the safety of Washington, to guard the line of the Potomac from Harper's Ferry to Alexandria, and protect Manassas Junction and the line of communications thence to the capital. It was essential, whether a direct or turning line of advance were selected, for McClellan to be secure while engaged in his operations, so that the Confederates should not be able to leave a containing force in front of him, and sending their main force into the Shenandoah Valley to carry the war into the Federals' country with the corresponding advantage to themselves which he proposed to gain by operating in Southern Virginia.

MOBILITY AND TRAINING.

In this war is brought out, also, the necessity for mobility. This was the basis of the success of the Confederates in the early years. They had less men than the Federals, and yet they were for a long time successful because, by means of rapid movement, they were able to bring superior numbers to decisive points. This mobility will always win wars. In the future, one reads, it will be sought by mechanical means, which must help to bring our troops by air, over or under seas, and overland to the decisive position before the enemy can reach it, and that battles stretching over areas of country will be directed by wireless from the air or from moving armoured headquarters manœuvring mobile bodies protected by armour and able to fire guns and machine guns.

Regulations teach us that we must learn from past experience, and that it is necessary to build on the past in order to make the future secure. The chief lesson, then, to be applied must be the improvement of our mobility, so that aircraft, seacraft, and motor vehicles are employed to add to it. Napoleon's orders were, before one of his battles, *activité, activité, vitesse*. Jackson's brigade, by marching 245 miles in thirty-five days, was able to win four battles and to influence the Federal plans of campaign, so that they failed to gain a decision at that time in spite of their advantages in man power, reserves, sea power, and wealth.

The skilful use that Jackson made of the obstacle of the Massanutton Mountains, parallel to his lines of operations, was largely due to the mobility of his force. This mobility was helped by the fact that his troops carried little with them, usually taking a blanket, waterproof sheet, haversack, and, if necessary, two days' rations. Trains were reduced to a minimum, and were often left behind, the troops living on the country. They always bivouacked and took no tents with them. Thus his troops were able at times to make forced marches. For instance, his force marched over fifty miles, from Front Royal to the River Potomac, in forty-eight hours, Again, on May 30th, his force marched twenty-five miles, and on the next day part of his force marched thirty-five miles, while the whole force marched twenty-eight miles. His mobility enabled him constantly to concentrate superior numbers at the decisive point, although his opponent, in the vicinity of the battle area, was much the stronger. For instance, at the battle of McDowell, May 8th, 1862, Jackson had 6,000 men opposed to the Federals' 2,500, though the latter had available 25,000 men. At Winchester, fought on May 25th, 1862, Jackson had 16,000 men, the Federals had 6,400 out of the 21,000 men available in the area of operations. At Port Republic, June 9th, 1862, he had 7,000 men to oppose the Federal 4,000 out of 47,000 available men if they had been properly concentrated.

In the future our mobility will not depend on the marching powers of man and horse, but on leaders, who have learnt to exploit as fully and as early as possible the mobility of all troops, mechanized and adequately armed, working in combination with aircraft and with the latest chemical inventions. The Commander must have trained leaders and troops ready to act in accordance with his ideas. General Jackson had to train his troops after the outbreak of war. His personality overcame the many difficulties of their lack of discipline and want of knowledge.

To-day these two points need not be considered if training is on the right lines. If, in the next two decades, we can train our forces to be mechanically mobile and to realize the necessity for altered conditions, we shall not have to fear the result.

If all ranks can be trained to meet the requirements of the rank above them, and if all who have to teach can be taught how and what to teach, and if the teaching is to think about the future in terms of progress, then there is the possibility that the existing small forces will again be capable of expansion in time of necessity and will be able to take their places in every variety of armoured gas-proof land cruisers. These can be manœuvred to the decisive place where, in combination with the latest scientific devices, they will be able to deal successfully with a less ready enemy.

This campaign brings out the value of sound military training for the leaders. Generals Lee and Jackson made full use of their available resources owing to their own skill and knowledge in applying the principles of war.

Secrecy of movement, mobility, surprise, economy of force, maintenance of the objective, and offensive action were abundantly illustrated during the campaign. Though the Federals had the opportunity of successfully making use of exterior lines and of concentrating superior numbers against the Confederates, yet so skilfully did the southern generals make use of their smaller forces on interior lines that they held off northern detachments and defeated other portions.

In addition to their military skill and zeal, their concentration on essentials, and their thoroughness in all details connected with their profession, these two Southern Commanders possessed the outstanding moral qualities of self-reliance, determination, and sincerity in their cause, which gave confidence to their men and brought success for a considerable time.

Able strategy, combined with sound tactics, enabled the weaker side to defer the result for many years and to gain many brilliant victories.

BIBLIOGRAPHY.

The following authorities have been consulted in compiling these notes : —

> Henderson's " Stonewall Jackson."
> Hamley's " Operations of War."
> Allan's " Valley Campaign."
> Kellogg's " Shenandoah Valley."

It would be difficult to recommend Colonel Henderson's book too strongly. The criticism that his hero has received a disproportionate share of praise in the Campaign at the expense of his Commander-in-Chief may at times be justified. But if the doings of Jackson had been chronicled with less sympathy, with less insight, and with less feeling, the book would have lost its very great charm.

In addition to the sound military advice and the astute deductions from and criticisms of engagements and battles, the portrait given of General Jackson is absorbingly interesting, and is finely sketched.

The author has entered so thoroughly into the spirit of the times and into the feelings of the General that one lives in the atmosphere, as one is made to see clearly how this rigid, honourable character influenced the cause to which he was devoted. One realizes what can be done by a man whose mind is trained to think on sound lines and whose character has been moulded, so that his actions are an example and an inspiration to those whom he has to lead. Colonel Henderson shows us Jackson as a stern fanatic suspending from duty an officer who broke the letter of an order in using his own boundary fence for firewood; as an exacting general forgetful that the rank and file had not the same interest in or knowledge of operations, and were consequently not buoyed up with his enthusiasm; and, again, as a man of intense purpose, sharing with simplicity and humility the hardships of his troops, and in consequence gaining their affection. Moral factors are paramount features in war. Jackson's presence on the field induced confidence in all ranks and added to their determination to gain a victory at all costs.

In this respect he may be favourably compared with the greatest of commanders, with the added quality of disinterested and self-sacrificing devotion to duty.

POLICY AND STRATEGY.

For political reasons the Confederates made a defensive plan, as their object was to show that they had no wish to be aggressive, and that they only wished to be independent. Also their population of seven million whites and three and a half half million blacks in the eleven States which seceded from the North had not the necessary superiority in numbers, material, and resources to justify the assumption of the offensive against all the Northern and North-Eastern States. The Federal militia and volunteers were well equipped, and they had a regular army of 16,000 men, and they had more numerous and more powerful artillery.

The Federals were helped not only by their numerical superiority, but by their naval superiority, and by the geography of the area of operations. By their sea power they had the advantage of an extensive base; they could move their bases; they could blockade the Confederate ports and could separate the combatants if they held the Mississippi. McClellan during the Seven Days' Battle changed his base. When his army was astride the Chickahominy and was struck at Gaines' Mill, he was saved only by his command of the sea. The Confederates could not tell where the Federals would next strike a blow. This added to their difficulties and to the fog of war. Command of the sea also induced detachments.

The geography of the country enabled them to strike at the Confederate capital by the Shenandoah Valley from Harper's Ferry; from Washington by the Orange and Alexandria Railway via Alexandria, Bristow, Warrenton Junction, Culpepper Court House, Gordonsville; from the River Potomac, using the Richmond-Fredericksburg Railway at Acquia Creek via Ashland; from Fort Munroe by the road running north-west; or from the River James via Harrison's Landing and Petersburg, then north via Drewry's Bluff.

All these lines of advance were used, and owing to the secrecy gained by sea power, they were able to obtain the advantage of massing superior numbers at the decisive points in each of their advances. A Federal advance up the River James did not force the Confederates to form front parallel to their communications, as Richmond, twenty miles from White House and twenty-five miles from Harrison's Landing, commanded the approaches from these places.

However, their sea power gave the Federals considerable choice in their lines of advance; also it added to the Confederates' difficulties in gaining a decisive victory. When defeated, the Federals could withdraw to their base and re-embark if necessary.

On September 1st, 1862, when Pope's defeated army was at Centreville, Jackson's Corps moved round his northern flank. Had Pope not been able to withdraw to his entrenched base on the Potomac at Alexandria, the result might have been decisive. He could even then have withdrawn further to his ships at Acquia Creek.

The difficulties of the Federals, however, were to maintain themselves when they had landed. The Confederates had excellent inter-communication by means of their railways, which enabled them to move troops rapidly either laterally or from the north to south. These railways were mainly useful as lines of supply. By the Manassas Railway troops and supplies could be moved from Woodstock to Strasburg and Salem, then through Thorofare Gap to Manassas Junction; from Staunton they could be moved over the Blue Ridge via Gordonsville to Richmond and White House; from Lynchburg they could be moved east to Petersburg and then up via Richmond and Fredericksburg to Acquia Creek, and north via Orange Court House and Fairfax to Bristow. Thus, when McClellan advanced on Richmond from White House, he was threatened with envelopment on his northern flank by the advance of Jackson, who reached Hanover from the Valley. He thereupon transferred his base to the River James in order to prevent this and to cover his base. As the railways were in the hands of the Confederates, the Federals had long and costly transport trains.

These were vulnerable, and decreased the Federals' mobility in the plain east of the Blue Ridge, where roads were bad, forest and swamps were numerous, and the Potomac, Rappahannock, Mattapomy, Pamunkey, James, Appomattox, and Shenandoah rivers were considerable obstacles. This consequently added to the duration of the war and to the Federals' difficulties in reaching their first objective—viz., the Confederate capital. They had planned to gain an early and decisive success by the capture of Richmond.

McClellan's difficulties were increased by the fact that his Government did not wholeheartedly support his plans, and that the conduct of his operations was on double and exterior lines. He was constantly hampered in his strategical arrangements by political interference. Whenever the Federal capital was threatened by an advance up the Shenandoah Valley, McClellan was diverted from carrying out his main objective.

It is a much-discussed question as to how far the statesman can take a part in the conduct of war. Lincoln considered that it would have been fatal to McClellan when he was trying to gain a decisive victory if the Confederates had raided and burnt down Washington, and so he moved troops to ensure the safety of his capital. It was on this point that Lincoln and McClellan disagreed.

On the one hand, McClellan did not take sufficient pains to explain situations and to allay the statesman's fear; on the other hand, the President did not understand strategy. A Commander-in-Chief has to remember that his actions must be influenced by Government policy and by considerations of finance, and that the statesman has to make certain that they receive due attention. The statesman has to keep in mind the fact that, though he is competent to appreciate the general principles of the projects of operations laid down before him, yet he should not, owing to insufficient military training, attempt to frame a plan himself or to take a part in the conduct of the campaign.

In March, '62, five separate commands were instituted by Lincoln, and army corps commanders were appointed without reference to the Commander-in-Chief. The many withdrawals of McDowell and the attempts to intercept Jackson in the Shenandoah Valley were most hampering to the effective conduct of operations. It was not till 1864 that the military commander was allowed to carry out his operations unfettered by political interference. Then there was unity of effort with all resources combined for the single aim of defeating the Confederate field forces. General Grant thus soon attained his purpose. The Confederate President made mistakes chiefly of policy. He insisted on a defensive strategy.

GEOGRAPHY.

The geography in the area of operations affected the strategy of the campaign. The valley of the River Shenandoah, a tributary of the River Potomac, which joins that river at Harper's Ferry, lies between the Alleghanies and the Blue Mountains. It is 120 miles long, with an average breadth of twenty-four miles, enclosed on either side by steep and rocky mountains about 3,000 feet high, covered with forest and traversable only at the gaps. The chief passes over the Blue

Mountains are Foster's Gap, Snicker's Gap, Ashby's Gap, Manassas Gap, which crosses an outlying ridge known as Bull Run Mountains at Thorofare, Fisher's, Thornton's, Swift Run, Semans, Brown's and Jaman Gaps. An excellent metalled road joined Winchester and Staunton, passing through Harrisonburg, Newmarket, Mount Jackson and Strasburg.

From Staunton the road crosses the Middle and North rivers by wooden bridges before reaching Harrisonburg.

Small tracks run parallel to this main road for the greater part of its length. From Newmarket a metalled road leads across the Massanutton Mountains, crosses the South Fork at White House Bridge, passes Luray, and crosses the Blue Ridge by Thornton's Gap to Sperryville and Culpepper. An unpaved road runs down the Luray Valley from Port Republic to Front Royal, and from this latter point a good road leads to Winchester, and country roads to Strasburg, Middleton, and other places on the Valley turnpike. From Winchester good metalled roads lead to Harper's Ferry and through Martinsburg to Williamsport on the River Potomac. Away from the metalled roads it was difficult to move an army with its guns and wagons. The lower portions of the Shenandoah Valley are well timbered; the surface is undulating, with no steep slopes. Round Winchester there are large fields, divided by low stone walls. Elsewhere the country was open and intersected by numerous channels, which are liable to sudden floods. The Shenandoah river flows between steep banks. Near Front Royal it divides into two parts, known as the North and South Forks, flowing on either side of the Massanuttons. These mountains can only be crossed by an army by the Newmarket-Luray road. Near Port Republic the South Fork is split into three streams, called the North, Middle and South rivers. The valley east of the Massanuttons is only ten miles wide, traversed by a single unmetalled road. The Western Valley, up which the North Fork flows, is more open, and is better adapted for the movement of troops.

The valley of the Shenandoah played a most important part in the war. It gave a covered approach on to the Federal communications and threatened Washington, which was separated only by the River Potomac from Virginia. It afforded an excellent line of approach to Maryland, and one which, if the Confederates held the mountain passes on either side, was practically safe from interference. It was also a most useful source of supply. The possession of the passes over the Blue Ridge Mountains was of more importance to the Confederates than to the Federals. They thus acquired the power of debouching from them on their enemy's line of communications, and could ensure their own safety while advancing against Maryland. The Federals could gain little by transferring their main operations to the western side of the Blue Ridge, for in their case, although threatening the Confederate line of communications with the west, it led only by an indirect route to their objective—the Confederate capital. Detachments in the Valley were necessary for the Confederates, as they relieved the pressure on Richmond and contained greatly superior numbers.

JACKSON'S OPERATIONS.

Jackson, with some 17,000 men, contained Banks with 20,000, McDowell with 40,000, Frémont with 14,000, and 7,000 were kept at Harper's Ferry. Had the Confederates, who were forced to carry out a defensive strategy, kept all their troops concentrated in one position, the task of the Federals would have been simplified. They could in turn have concentrated. They would have been in no doubt as to where the decisive place was, and they could have taken sufficient time to obtain superior numbers.

The fighting in the Valley, therefore, became an important strategic counterstroke.

The Confederates were in a large salient.

The obstacle of the Massanutton Mountains screened Jackson's march to Front Royal from Banks, who was at Strasburg. Frémont and Shields, marching on either side of these mountains, did not co-operate.

Jackson acted on interior lines against their divided forces. With 13,000 he was able to defeat 25,000 men in detail. On June 8th, at the Battle of Cross Keys, Frémont, with 12,000, was defeated by Ewell with half that number. On the following day this force was contained, and Jackson defeated Shields. Neither of the Federal forces helped the other during the operations. They were separated by the obstacle of the River Shenandoah.

On July 11th, 1861, the River Bull Run affected the strategy of the battle. The Federal commander planned an enveloping movement against the Confederates in position south of the river. When he sent a force to the south of the Bull Run, it became a detachment. The two parts of the Federal forces could be dealt with separately. Beauregard could either have crossed the river and struck at the Federals' left flank and communications along the Centreville-Warrenton road—this would have been decisive if successful—or he could have attacked the exposed detachment of Heintzlemann's 3rd and Hunter's 2nd divisions via Sudley Springs. The latter course was adopted and was completely successful owing to the excellent tactics of Stonewall Jackson and to the timely intervention of Kirby Smith's fresh brigade.

LEADERSHIP AND CIVILIAN INTERFERENCE.

An important point to be noted in this campaign is leadership. The early successes of the Confederates were due to their operations being under one control.

On the one side there was the Federal President directing operations, and on the other side there were trained soldiers and capable leaders. Lincoln's interference in the strategy and operations led to numbers being withdrawn from decisive points and to attacks against the Confederate Field Army not being made in the greatest possible strength.

Lincoln's anxiety for the safety of Washington caused him to withdraw troops from McClellan and to depart from his original plans.

Lincoln had done all he could to prepare for a successful war, but he did realize that detachments made for the defence of the capital reduce the fighting strength, and that if the enemy are free to manœuvre, they can concentrate against the forces allotted for defence. He did not realize that it is best to defeat the enemy's main army and then the capital will be in no danger from it. By constantly changing his plans, he did not realize that he allowed his opponent time to add to his resources and to his fighting strength, reduced the possibilities of surprise and of gaining the initiative for his army. He did not understand that, by making separate commands, he was dissipating his forces so completely that co-operation in a common action and concentration of force were impossible, and that his procrastination gave opportunities which led to successes and a consequent raising of his enemy's *morale*.

He conformed to the plans of the Confederates, and so, until he handed over the control to General Grant, there could be no final victory for the Federals in spite of their enormous resources in men, ships, supplies, and money.

COMPARISON OF NUMBERS ON BOTH SIDES.

The Confederates in the spring of 1862 could place 60,000 men in the field out of their population of seven million white men to oppose 30,000 men of the Federal Army in West Virginia, 30,000 south of the River Potomac, and 150,000 available to land on the east coast for operations against Richmond. The population of the North was twenty million whites.   By the end of 1861 the Federal Navy had 264 ships. In three years' time these numbers were more than doubled.

On both sides there was a great lack of discipline among junior commanders and troops, and on both sides staff work failed on important occasions.

RAIDS.

Raids played an important part in this campaign.   It is essential that they should be carried out with secrecy and rapidity.   They can, however, never be decisive.   They may cause inconvenience and lower an enemy's *morale*, but they cannot seriously affect a result.   They must be relevant to the main situation.

PERSONNEL AND ARMAMENT.

As regards personnel on both sides, the infantry formed up in lines covered by scouts.   When in close contact the scouts became part of the front line.   The area of operations was wooded, so both sides made use of concealed positions protected with trunks of trees, cut down and piled up, or of trenches without head-cover.

All the fighting was done at close range, as the decisive range of their muzzle-loading rifles was 250 yards and their guns were not effective beyond 2,000 yards.   The companies were about thirty-five strong, and there were ten companies to a battalion, three or four brigades to a division.   The Federals, except at Fredericksburg, were organized into divisions.   The Confederates were organized at their big battles into corps, each of four or five divisions.   These divisions were up to 12,000 strong.   General Jackson's division consisted of three infantry brigades under Winder, Campbell and Taliaferro respectively.   In General Ewell's division were four brigades, commanded by Taylor, Trimble Elzey and Scott respectively.   The Confederate cavalry was commanded by Stuart and Ashby.

Operations on both sides were affected by the lack of discipline and training.   Straggling on the march and pillaging after battles were prevalent.   Fire discipline was defective. Outpost duties were often neglected.   The cavalry fought as mounted infantry, as they were not armed with swords and lances, but with revolvers or rifles.   The Confederates had an advantage in this arm.

The majority of them had experience in dealing with horses and in riding.   It was for this reason that they enjoyed a greater security during the operations and fuller knowledge as to dispositions and movements than the Federals did. For instance, in May, 1862, when Jackson was advancing to Harper's Ferry, his 16,000 men were exaggerated into double the numbers by the Federals' reports.   In both armies the system of replenishing supplies and ammunition was faulty, and led to men leaving their firing positions to obtain cartridges and to leaving the ranks on the march to get food. These breaches of discipline led Lord Wolseley to express the opinion that " a single army corps of regular soldiers would have turned the scale in favour of either side."

CHAPTER II.

A STUDY OF THE STRATEGY AND TACTICS OF THE SHENANDOAH VALLEY CAMPAIGN, TO JUNE 17TH, 1862.

Illustrating the Principles of War.

Diary of Events.

1860.

December 20th.—South Carolina dissolved their union from the other States.

December 26th.—Fort Moultrie was seized by the people of South Carolina.

1861.

February.—Six other States in which cotton was grown with slave labour seceded. Jefferson Davis was elected President of the Confederate Government.

March 4th.—Abraham Lincoln, the Republican candidate, became President. His election had turned on the question of slavery.

April 8th.—Orders were given by the Confederates that Fort Sumter, a port of South Carolina in Charleston Harbour, garrisoned by Federals, was to be reduced.

April 12th.—The artillery of this Southern State opened fire on the fort. This was the first open act of rebellion.

April 13th.—Fort Sumter surrendered to General Beauregard. No lives were lost on either side, but this action started the Civil War. Virginia, North Carolina, Tennessee and Arkansas were definitely brought into the Southern Confederacy. Maryland and Kentucky wavered at first, but were eventually saved to the Union. Missouri became the seat of a local guerilla warfare.

April 15th.—President Lincoln called out 75,000 three months' militia of the Northern States to suppress the rebellion in the South.

April 17th.—Virginia seceded from the Union in preference to furnishing the troops required by President Lincoln. The governing bodies in this State held that the action of the Confederates in enforcing the withdrawal of Federal troops from one of their States was legitimate.   They decided to resist coercion in any detail of the interior administration of States, and they could not contribute to the troops which the North required for maintaining the Union by force.   It was this attitude of resistance that caused the Confederates at the beginning of the war to adopt a defensive policy.

April 29th.—Jackson, as Colonel of Virginia volunteers, was given command of the troops at Harper's Ferry.   This was a force of cavalry, artillery and infantry, numbering 4,500 men. He was opposed by 14,000 Federals under General Patterson on the northern bank.   Harper's Ferry was important, as it covered Winchester and the main route running south via Kernstown, Newmarket to Staunton.

May 3rd.—Lincoln increased his available forces to 150,000 men.

May 24th.—General Johnston assumed command of the Confederate garrison now increased to 10,000 men at Harper's Ferry.   Jackson was given the command of the First Brigade of the Army of the Shenandoah.   This brigade consisted of five Virginia infantry regiments and one battery of artillery. The main Confederate Army of 20,000 men under General Beauregard was stationed at Manassas Junction.   This was an important railway centre of Northern Virginia.   Four Federal regiments crossed the River Potomac and took up a position on the Arlington Heights, in order to protect Washington from the west.

June 1st.—A force of 25,000 Federals was in position on the northern boundaries of North-West Virginia.

June 14th.—General Johnston destroyed the railway bridge over the River Potomac.

June 15th.—General Johnston's force retired towards Winchester.   General Patterson's force marched through Maryland and occupied Williamsport.

June 20th.—Workshops of the Baltimore and Ohio Railway were destroyed by men of Jackson's Brigade at Martinsburg.

July 2nd.—Patterson's force crossed the River Potomac. Jackson's Brigade checked Patterson's advanced guard in a rearguard action at Falling Waters.   Richmond became the Confederate capital.

July 3rd.—Patterson's force advanced to Martinsburg. Fourth Congress passed a vote for 500,000 men and 500 million dollars to be provided for the war against the South.

July 7th.—Johnston withdrew to Winchester. The Federal Army at Washington was now 50,000 men. It was commanded by General McDowell. A portion of this army was south of the River Potomac threatening Beauregard's Army while a portion advanced towards Staunton.

July 11th.—McClellan defeated the Confederate troops at Rich Mountain.

July 13th.—McClellan defeated the Confederate troops at Carrick's Ford.

The Confederate Army now consisted of the Army of the Potomac, 28,000 men, including some cavalry and 29 guns, and the Shenandoah Valley Army, consisting of some cavalry, 4 infantry brigades, and 22 guns.

McDowell's Federal Army opposite Manassas Junction consisted of 14 brigades, divided among five divisions, seven cavalry troops, and 49 guns.

Although in the summer of 1861 the Federals had been successful in the desultory operations in Maryland and West Virginia, the Confederates under Johnston held the Shenandoah Valley and occupied Manassas. It was the object of McDowell, who commanded the Union troops round Washington, to defeat and drive back Beauregard from Manassas, while Patterson had to carry out a similar operation against Johnston, who held Winchester, after having captured Harper's Ferry.

July 15th.—Patterson's force advanced on Winchester.

July 17th.—Patterson moved on Charlestown instead of attacking Johnston's Shenandoah Army, in order to prevent them from joining their main force at Bull Run, where McDowell meant to make an attack against the main Confederate Army.

General Johnston, commanding the Shenandoah Army, contained the Federal forces under Patterson in this area with Stuart's troops.

July 18th.—The 1st Confederate Brigade, commanded by Jackson, began its march to Manassas Junction through Winchester and Ashby's Gap.

July 19th.—Stuart's cavalry joined the three Confederate brigades (Jackson's, Bee's, Bartow's), now marching to entrain at Piedmont, *en route* for Beauregard.

Patterson, in the Valley, was not aware that the Confederate Shenandoah Army was not in his front.

Jackson's Brigade entrained at Piedmont and reached Manassas Junction.

July 20th.—McDowell spent the day in reconnaissance of the fords over the river and in making his plans. Sudley Ford, two miles north-west of Stone Bridge, on the Centreville-Groveton road, was discovered.

BATTLE OF FIRST BULL RUN, JULY 21ST.

The Federals, commanded by McDowell, were 35,000 strong, consisting of five divisions, seven troops of cavalry, and 49 guns.

The Confederates, posted on the western bank of the River Potomac, were 28,000 strong, in which were 2,500 cavalry and 29 guns. They occupied a position on a front of six miles between Union Mills and the Warrenton Turnpike. The Shenandoah troops were in reserve, the remainder of Beauregard's Army held the crossings.

The Confederates' offensive operations on their right flank were delayed owing to the necessary orders not being received by brigades.

Two Federal divisions, therefore, who had been ordered to turn the Confederates' left, crossed Sudley Ford two and a half miles north-west of the Turnpike road.

The Federals were checked by the nearest brigade at Stone Bridge sending troops to take up a position at Matthew's Hill west of the Bull Run river. The Federals were not able to exploit their success with their reserves, before the Confederates were able to swing back their left flank to the Henry House Hill and take up a position suitable for defence.

The Federals' easterly frontal attacks were met by Jackson's Brigade. No attempt by the Federals was made to advance over Stone Bridge and take the Confederates' flank position in reverse.

At 2.45 p.m., after the Federals' turning force had repeatedly attacked without success, Jackson's Brigade counter-attacked, and was joined on his left flank by Kirby Smith's 1900 bayonets, which had recently arrived by train at Manassas Junction Station. Reserve brigades of Bee, Hampton, and Evans advanced on Jackson's right flank.

The Federals did not attempt to bring up their reserve divisions. Their three divisions engaged in the critical fighting on the Henry House Hill totalled 18,000 men with 30 guns. The seven Confederate brigades were thus able to oppose them in equal strength on the Henry House Hill with only nine guns less than the Federals.

Though the Federals made a final stand at Young's Branch, Early's Brigade was brought up and again attacked their right. The Federals now broke and retired in disorder across the Bull Run.   Then their routed and demoralized forces withdrew within the defences of Washington.

Confederate troops crossed at McLean's Ford and at Union Mill, and turned their immediate retreat into a rout.   The main Confederate Army followed slowly to Centreville. There was no organized and sustained pursuit.   The Federals lost 1,500 men killed and wounded and 25 guns and 1,300 prisoners; the Confederates lost 1,982 men.

The Confederates did not follow up their success, though even the Federals considered that the fall of Washington was inevitable, if there had been a pursuit after this battle, as nothing had been done to man or guard the approaches to the city.

The Confederate troops, however, were too much disorganized and scattered after their victory to follow up McDowell's Army, and throughout the rest of the year and until the spring of 1862, although they occupied the country round Manassas Junction and Centreville and fortified their position, they made no further advance, but, like the Federals, spent the interval in consolidating their forces and improving their defences.

It has been reported that President Davis would not allow an advance on Washington for reasons of policy.   He did not wish to be considered aggressive.

The Confederates in separating from the Union merely wished to be independent, and they did not wish to conquer and occupy other territory or impose their will on other States. Therefore, President Davis did not consider that it would have been wise to invade the Federal country.

This Confederate victory relieved the pressure on the province of Virginia.   The defeat roused the North and made them realize the necessity for a large army and navy. Congress authorized an army of 500,000 men.

Both sides were active throughout the autumn.

November 1st.—McClellan succeeded Scott as Commander of the Federal Army.

Johnston's Army of Northern Virginia remained at Centreville.   This army was 40,000 strong and was organized in two Corps.   Johnston's plan for the invasion of the United States was not sanctioned by President Davis.

The Federal President would not allow McClellan to carry out his combined operations with the Navy bombarding the Confederate ports on the Atlantic and in the Gulf of Mexico, and with the Army advancing through Virginia, Carolina, and Georgia.

The Federal Government, however, completed the blockade

of the Confederate ports. Had they carried out the full plan and secured New Orleans and the Mississippi, they would have struck at a vital point.

November 4th.—Stonewall Jackson was appointed to command the Shenandoah Valley District, *i.e.*, the country between the Blue Ridge Mountains and the backbone of the Alleghanies. The campaign had not been favourable during the summer and autumn to the South. The Federals had gained control of the greater part of Virginia west of the mountains and north of the Great Kanawha river, and had pushed their outposts into and beyond the mountain range. Kelly occupied Romney with 5,000 men; another force was at Bath, while the north bank of the River Potomac was everywhere guarded by Union troops, approximately 25,000 strong, in the Mountain District. Jackson's headquarters were at Winchester. His force of 4,000 men was opposed by about 37,000 men, separated in detachments at Grafton, Clarksburg, on the Ohio, and on the line of communications.

The Shenandoah Valley was an important theatre of operations during the war, as, by holding the mountain passes on either side, it was safe from flank incursions, it afforded a source of supply, and was a covered line of advance to Maryland. From the Blue Ridge Mountains the Confederates could strike at the Federals' communications. It was not on the direct line of advance to Richmond, which was the Federals' objective, and so they did not consider the advantage of laying it waste, as was done in 1864.

December 6th-9th.—Jackson's troops destroyed Dam No. 5, on the Chesapeake and Ohio Canal.

December 25th.—General Loring's brigades came under Jackson's command at Winchester. His force was now 10,000 infantry, 600 cavalry, and 26 guns. He decided to attack the Federals before they received reinforcements.

1862.

January 1st.—Jackson's Army left Winchester, advancing north on Martinsburg, towards Bath. Jackson first of all wished to regain West Virginia. The plan he recommended for this purpose was to advance by the roads parallel to the Baltimore-Ohio Railway from the north-east, in order to cut the Federals' communications, and force them to evacuate or fight under unfavourable circumstances. His first move was to march on Romney, guarding his flank towards the north by detachments and striking the railway at New Creek. To carry out this plan, he asked for the return of his Stonewall Brigade, which had been left at Manassas, and that the troops operating along the line of the Alleghanies south-west of Winchester should be put under his command.

January 4th.—Jackson's troops reached Bath. Although the Federals were not surprised and the outflanking operations of the Confederates were not synchronized, yet they vacated the town. Confederates captured much-needed stores.

The position and forces of the Federal Army at the beginning of 1862 were as follows: —

Rosecrans (later replaced by Frémont), commanding the troops in the Mountain District, had 22,000 men in Western Virginia, whom he was concentrating on the Baltimore-Ohio Railway under cover of 5,000 men, commanded by Kelly, who occupied Romney. His intention was to advance as early as possible and seize Winchester, in order to cover the north-eastern and central parts of Western Virginia and to threaten the left of the Confederates' position about Centreville. Banks' V Corps headquarters, in quarters at Frederick, had 16,000 men with detachments guarding the River Potomac from Harper's Ferry to Williamsport.

January 5th.—Jackson's troops severed the communications of the Federals between Frederick and Romney by the destruction of a railway bridge across the Cacapon river.

January 7th.—Jackson withdrew twelve miles south of Bath to Ungers Store. The weather was very severe, so that Jackson found it necessary to halt for some days at Ungers to rest his troops and rough-shoe his horses. In order to mislead the enemy as to his intention of marching on Romney, he sent small forces towards Moorefield and Bath. The Federals in the vicinity retreated on Patterson's Creek to the railway.

January 13th.—Jackson resumed his march to Romney. General Kelly had evacuated this place.

January 14th.—Jackson, having left Loring's militia at Romney to watch the Federals at Cumberland, started on his return to Winchester with Garnett's Brigade. A brigade of militia was extended as far as Moorefield, keeping touch with Johnson on the Alleghany Mountains, another militia brigade was stationed at Bath, and a third at Martinsburg. His troops at Winchester were in a position to resist Banks or to support Loring if necessary.

January 24th.—Jackson's force, 4,600 strong, reached Winchester. His operations had accomplished their strategical objective. His enemy were now north of the River Potomac. He then placed them on the defensive, and had dispersed the troops opposing him from Cumberland to Frederick on a front of eighty miles.

He secured a valuable recruiting area and a base for further supplies in Virginia.

January 30th.—The Confederate Secretary for War ordered Jackson to withdraw Loring from Romney, as he considered that his troops might be cut off if left at this place.   They were a detachment two days' march from Jackson's present position.

January 31st.—Jackson disagreed with the decision as to Loring's recall.   He also considered that this civilian interference was unjustifiable.   He therefore resigned his position in command of the Shenandoah Army.

This resignation was subsequently withdrawn.   Loring was removed from Jackson's command and took all the non-Virginian regiments with him.   The Federals, finding that the Confederates had withdrawn, recrossed the river and occupied Romney, repairing the bridge across the River Cacapon, and reopening the railway from the West to Hancock.

February.—During this month Johnston's Army of Northern Virginia, 47,000 strong, remained at Centreville and Manassas Junction.   McClellan's Army of the Potomac was at Washington over 200,000 strong.

February 24th.—The Federals, under Banks, advanced into the Shenandoah Valley.

February 27th.—General Banks, commanding three divisions, 38,000 men, including 2,000 cavalry, with 80 guns, crossed the River Potomac at Harper's Ferry.   Jackson's Army could now be threatened in rear by General Frémont's force moving on Staunton from Beverley.

March 7th.—General D. H. Hill withdrew from Leesburg. Banks reached Stephenson's Depot.

March 8th.—The Confederate ship *Merrimac* sank two Federal ships in the River James.

March 9th.—General Johnston withdrew to the vicinity of Orange Court House, south of the Rapidan.   He was thus in a central position from which he could reach the Valley at Staunton via the Virginia Central Railway, or Strasburg via the Manassas Railway, or south-east to Richmond by the Orange and Alexandria Railway.

A Federal ironclad silenced the *Merrimac.*

March 10th.—Jackson was now in an isolated position in the Shenandoah Valley with 3,600 infantry, 600 cavalry, and 27 guns.   The position of the Federal troops was as follows:

Schenk had 3,000 men at Cumberland and Romney.   Kelly

had 4,000 and two batteries at Petersburg, and on the railway. Milroy had 6,000 and three batteries at Cheat Mountains. Cox had 12,000 and two batteries at Kanawha River.

The main duty of these troops spread over a considerable area was to guard the communications and to keep down any hostile movements by the inhabitants.

March 11th.—Jackson withdrew from Winchester to Mount Jackson. The Federals occupied Berryville. Jackson, commanding 3,600 infantry, 600 cavalry and 27 guns, abandoned Winchester, although he realized its strategic value, because Banks, with two divisions, under Shields and Williams, of approximately 10,000 men each, was moving against him with superior numbers, and because Johnston's retirement southwards from Centreville in the first week of March had left him isolated.   In addition, he wished to draw as many Federals as possible up the Valley, so that thereby McClellan's main army might be weakened.

Banks' leading troops occupied Strasburg.

March 12th.—General McClellan was confined in his command to the Potomac Army.

Jackson's force reached Strasburg on this day.   Banks sent forward Shields' Division.   During Jackson's withdrawal, Ashby, with 500 sabres and three guns, not only formed a screen to cover the Confederate forces, but constantly harassed the enemy's flanks, and, skirmishing with them, deceived them as to the numbers and position of the withdrawing troops.

The retreat of the main Confederate Army behind the Rappahannock, in conjunction with Jackson's withdrawal to Mount Jackson, led the Federals to suppose that the latter could be neglected as being too weak to fight.   The pressure on Washington being removed, the greater portion of the Federal V Corps was, therefore, ordered to withdraw.

March 16th.—General Banks sent Shields' Division, 7,000 strong, including 750 cavalry and 24 guns, to Winchester, and Williams' Division to Manassas.

March 17th.—McClellan began to embark at Alexandria his force of 58,000 men and 100 guns for Fort Monroe.   This was to be accomplished in fifteen trips.   McClellan's plan was with his II, III and V Corps to advance along the Yorktown Peninsula on Richmond.   He meant to open up the York and James rivers with the co-operation of the Navy, in order to secure his flanks.   His I Corps was to turn the Confederate defences at Yorktown and Gloucester.

March 18th.—Shields' Division was sent forward to Strasburg.   Jackson was at Woodstock.

March 20th.—Williams' Division began to move to Manassas as a post of observation against the Confederates advancing from the south, while Shields' was ordered back to Strasburg.

March 21st.—Ashby reported to Jackson that the Federals were withdrawing from Winchester for Castlenau Ferry. In the Shenandoah Valley, Banks had one division retiring from Strasburg on Winchester, and another division was moving across the Blue Ridge, via Snicker's Gap, for Manassas Junction. Federal troops left the Shenandoah Valley for Manassas Junction, in order to fulfil the conditions of McClellan's scheme. McClellan's plan was to strike at the enemy in the West at Nashville, in Tennessee, and in the East at Richmond, and to attack points on the coast and on the Mississippi. For his march on Richmond he wanted to start from Urbanna on the Rappahannock river, but Johnston's sudden retirement on Gordonsville rendered such a course inadvisable. He was thus forced to operate up the Yorktown Peninsula from Fort Monroe. Jackson, hearing that the Federals were dispatching troops to strengthen the Army of the Potomac, now determined to stop this by a vigorous offensive.

March 22nd.—Ashby had a skirmish with Shields' outposts about a mile south of Winchester. He reported that he was in touch with remnants of the Federal troops—namely, four infantry regiments that had not yet withdrawn to Harper's Ferry.
Jackson's force marched twenty-two miles to Strasburg.

BATTLE OF KERNSTOWN.

March 23rd.—Jackson continued his advance, reaching Kernstown by 1 p.m., after a fourteen-mile march. The Confederates, numbering 3,400 infantry, 290 cavalry, and 27 guns, were defeated by Shields' Division on this day. Jackson's force was divided into three brigades, under Garnett, Banks and Fullerton. Shields' three brigades were under Tyler, Kimball and Sullivan.

Jackson's troops were very tired after their long marches, and then two-thirds of them had to carry out the arduous manœuvres of a turning movement to gain a position on the ridge which dominated the right flank of Shields' position.

It was on this ridge that the main battle took place. The Federals, with a superiority in numbers of 3,600 men, drove back the Confederates from this high ground.

When Jackson's main body reached the vicinity of

Kernstown, at first he intended to halt, as his troops were tired with their two days' march, but, believing that it would be dangerous to postpone his attack to the next day, as the Federals could see the strength of his force, he determined to attack.   Also he believed that the force opposed to him was much smaller than it really was, as Ashby, on March 21st, reported that only four regiments were in the vicinity and that these had been ordered to retire on Harper's Ferry.   Actually Shields had 750 sabres, 24 guns and 7,000 rifles ready to oppose the Confederates.   Shields ordered Kimball to take up a position with his brigade two miles north of Kernstown on the Strasburg-Winchester road.   Sullivan was ordered to take his brigade to support Kimball, covering the approaches by the way of the Cedar Creek, Front Royal, Berryville and Romney roads.

Tyler's Brigade and Broadhead's cavalry were kept in reserve.   At daylight on March 23rd, Jackson sent four companies of infantry to support Ashby at Kernstown, and shortly afterwards advanced with his whole force.   When Jackson's main body arrived at Kernstown, he found that Ashby's troops had been driven back by Kimball's and Sullivan's Brigades, and that these two Federal brigades were in position on either side of the main Winchester-Strasburg road, with guns posted on Pritchard's Hill.   The Federals' left flank was specially strong, owing to Ashby's demonstrations.   Jackson therefore determined to move against the Federals' right flank from the high ground, and by capturing it to make their whole position untenable.

He instructed Ashby to continue his demonstrations against the Federals' front while he marched on to the high ground with one brigade, followed by Garnett's with 16 guns.   He left another brigade near the main road to act as a support to Ashby, and as a general reserve.

The Confederate artillery was able to enfilade the Federal guns and to compel them to withdraw.   The first four Confederate battalions sent forward occupied a stone fence which ran down the west side of the ridge opposite a large wood, their guns being on the ridge itself.   Four more battalions reinforced the Confederate position, forming up on the right of those already there, and covering their guns with their right flank.

The Federal commander now realized the danger to his right wing, and sent up Tyler's Brigade with orders to attack the Confederates' left flank.   Tyler's first assault was repulsed about 3.30 p.m.   His subsequent attacks were also defeated. Six Federal battalions from their left flank were now brought up to help Tyler.   Jackson, too, made an effort to support his left flank, but the six Federal battalions caused his troops to fall back before the three Confederate battalions could come up, and Garnett, who commanded on the right flank of the Confederate position, where the situation was critical, ordered the troops to retire.   Their retreat was covered by two of the battalions sent forward to support the Confederate left flank, but the advancing Federals enveloped both flanks, pressed them back, and forced the whole Confederate force to withdraw.

The Federals lost 570; the Confederate losses were 700 and two guns.

The Confederates retired six miles to Newtown.   The Federals did not pursue, as there was no formed body in readiness, and there was considerable confusion and disorder in the units.

Owing to numerical disparity, Jackson could not expect to defeat the superior numbers of Federals.   Had the Federal General correctly appreciated the situation, he might have attacked down the main road in force.   Ashby's cavalry, supported by four companies in this area, would not have been strong enough to prevent Jackson's reserves and train from being overrun.   His line of retreat and communications would then have been in danger.   Kimball had sufficient troops to hold Jackson to his position on the high ground west of the main road.

The following points contributed to the Confederates' repulse at Kernstown, namely : —

(1) Ashby, the cavalry commander, giving Jackson incorrect information.

(2) Jackson's attacking force was less than half the numbers of the Federals.

(3) Jackson considered that the commander of the Stonewall Brigade was wrong in retiring instead of making a counter-attack.

The result of the battle was that President Lincoln diminished the strength of his fighting forces at the decisive point—namely, at Yorktown—in order to provide for the immediate safety of Washington.

McDowell's Corps of 40,000 men was halted at Manassas. Lincoln created the following commands : —McClellan in the Yorktown Peninsula, McDowell on the Rappahannock, Banks in the Shenandoah Valley, and Frémont in West Virginia.

March 26th.—Jackson's Army was between Woodstock and Mount Jackson.   The Federal Army was north of Tom's Brook.

March 29th.—Frémont succeeded Rosecrans in command of the Federal troops in the Mountain District.

April 2nd.—McClellan's force arrived at Fort Monroe. Banks' Division in the Valley crossed Tom's Brook and reached Edenburg.

By this date, Jackson had retired to Rude's Hill, destroying the bridges of the Manassas Railway as he withdrew. His position now was favourable for defence, and so here he proceeded to reorganize his troops. Ashby with the cavalry, supported by a brigade of infantry, held back the Federals at Stoney Creek, near Edenburg, to which point they had been compelled to retreat by Shields' advance.

The Federals expected to gain decisive results by the capture of the Confederate capital. The Federal Government now wished that Jackson's force should be driven from the Shenandoah Valley. Banks, however, was hampered by supply difficulties. His depots at Winchester were supplied by rail from Washington through Harper's Ferry. This railway was out of repair. The bridges were broken in the Manassas Gap Railway. He found great difficulty in dealing with the Massanuttons. If he advanced on both sides of this obstacle his force would be separated; if he was on one side only, his enemy might operate on the other side against his communications or rear.

April 5th.—McClellan, with 60,000 men, started to advance against the Confederate position between the York and James rivers, covering Yorktown. This position was held by 15,000 men under Magruder on a front of twelve miles.

April 10th.—Frémont from Western Virginia was in a position at Franklin from which he could strike across the Alleghany Mountains via Brock's Gap to Newmarket or Harrisonburg.

A Federal division at Manassas Junction was connected with Banks in the Shenandoah Valley by a brigade detached to Front Royal.

April 16th.—McClellan, with one division, attacked the Confederates on Warwick River, in order to control Dam No. 1 between Lee's and Wynne's Mills. This reconnaissance should have been useful to McClellan if it had been carried out vigorously. He made no further attempts to find out Lee's real strength.

This attempt to break through to Richmond failed.

April 17th.—Jackson withdrew to Harrisonburg.

April 19th.—Jackson by forced marches moved to Elk Run Valley, covering Swift Run Gap, leaving a detachment at Conrad's Store. Banks considered that Jackson had left the valley.

April 20th.—Johnson withdrew to West View, his front covered by the Shenandoah, his flanks resting on the mountains. Good roads led to his rear towards Gordonsville, where General Ewell's Division was within easy reach.

Retirement for Jackson was necessary, in order to avoid the danger of Banks crossing the Massanuttons at Newmarket and cutting the communications with Ewell by seizing Swift Run Gap. To carry out this operation, the Confederates marched over fifty miles in three days. So long as Jackson held this position, Banks, who had his main body about Harrisonburg, could not march to Staunton without exposing his flank and communications with the River Potomac, while, if he attacked Jackson and was defeated, he risked disaster in a difficult hostile country, his communications to Harper's Ferry being over a hundred miles long. Banks therefore decided to wait for the approach of Frémont's troops from the west before marching to Staunton.

April 21st.—Lee was appointed to command the Confederate forces in the field. He wrote to Jackson, suggesting the value of an attack on Banks, in order to divert the Federals from Fredericksburg. Jackson wished to get in rear of Banks by Newmarket or Harrisonburg if the latter advanced on Staunton.

April 29th.—Ewell's force of 8,500 men at Swift Run Gap, and E. Johnson's force of 2,800 men at Staunton were placed under General Jackson for operations in the Valley. Ewell's Division was in three brigades, under Taylor, Trimble and Elzey respectively. Jackson's brigades were now commanded by Winder, Campbell and Taliaferro. The other forces were disposed as follows on this date: Generals Johnston and Magruder at Yorktown opposed McClellan's 110,000. Anderson, with 12,000 at Fredericksburg, faced McDowell's 33,000. Between Winchester and Romney, Generals Blenker and Frémont had 12,000. Between Warrenton and Woodstock, Generals Abercrombie and Geary had 6,500 men. General Banks had 20,000 men at Harrisonburg; General Schenck had 3,300 at Franklin; General Milroy had 3,500 north-west of Staunton.

April 30th.—Ashby made demonstrations towards Harrisonburg. Jackson left his camp, which was occupied by Ewell. Banks, alarmed by Ewell's march into the Shenandoah Valley, withdrew to Newmarket, where he arrived by May 5th.

May 1st.—Federals captured New Orleans.

Jackson's Division marched only five miles, owing to excessive rains.

Banks, hearing that General Ewell had entered the Shenandoah Valley, and that Jackson was moving, gradually withdrew to Newmarket, as he was afraid that the combined forces of Ewell and Jackson would attack him.

The absence of Jackson in Western Virginia made President Lincoln less apprehensive than usual about the safety of Washington.   In reply, therefore, to McClellan's requests for reinforcements, he ordered McDowell to advance from Fredericksburg to co-operate with the main Federal army in the Yorktown Peninsula.

At the same time, he removed Shields' Division from Banks, leaving him only 8,000 men.

Shields was ordered to join McDowell.

May 3rd.—Jackson realized that Milroy, followed by Schenck, might unite with Banks or might interpose his force between Johnson and himself.   He therefore decided to join up with Johnson's Brigade and defeat Milroy.   Ewell, in the meantime, was to occupy the position he had left, in order to contain Banks.   Then he proposed to concentrate his forces to deal with Banks.   To carry out this plan, Jackson decided to march up the Shenandoah river to Port Republic, then to cross the Blue Ridge Mountains by Brown's Gap to Mechum's River Station, and thence reach Staunton.   The direction of his march was intended to deceive the Federals and to suggest that he was moving on Richmond.

President Lincoln halted McDowell's force at Fredericksburg.

Jackson's Division reached Mechum's Station.

May 4th.—Jackson's march was continued.   His artillery and trains marched to Staunton, the remainder of his division went by rail.

May 5th.—Jackson's Division was concentrated at Staunton.

May 7th.—Jackson started his march towards the Federal camp at McDowell, marching by the Staunton-Parkersburg road.   After passing the Harrisonburg road, Jackson struck General Milroy's outposts.   Milroy then ordered his force to concentrate at McDowell, where he prepared a defensive position.

Jackson's force bivouacked on Shaw's Fork.

BATTLE OF McDOWELL.

May 8th.—Jackson advanced north-west from Staunton towards positions held by Milroy and Schenck's Brigades, who formed the advanced guards of Frémont's force south and south-west of McDowell.

Jackson's force advanced up the Bull Run Pasture Mountain until Sitlington's Hill was reached. From this hill McDowell and the Federal camp could be commanded. Jackson's plan now was to halt for the day, and to send during the night of May 8th/9th the bulk of his artillery with an infantry escort by road to a point on the road leading to Monterey, five miles west of McDowell. He intended to contain Milroy frontally while he cut off his retreat.

However, before midday on May 8th, Schenck joined Milroy and approved of the plan to attack the Confederates.

At 4.30 p.m. Milroy's infantry, supported by guns from Hull's Hill and from south of the village, attacked Jackson's position on Sitlington Hill for four hours without success. Jackson brought up Taliaferro's and subsequently Campbell's Brigades to support his leading brigade, and was able to maintain his position throughout the day. McDowell was rendered untenable by the dominating position held by the Confederates. When the Federals withdrew, there was no immediate pursuit by the Confederates owing to the density of the country and owing to their lack of information as to the strength and dispositions of Frémont's force at Franklin.

May 12th.—Shields left the Shenandoah Valley. General Lee, commanding the Confederate Army, realized the necessity of stopping Banks from reinforcing either McDowell or McClellan, and of preventing Banks from cutting the Virginia Central Railway and the communications between Richmond and Western Virginia. He therefore urged Jackson to advance against Banks and to threaten the line of the River Potomac.

Banks retired to Strasburg, leaving 1,000 men under Kenly at Front Royal, to protect the railway and the bridges over the Shenandoah. The reason for this retirement was that Banks' force had now a strength of 8,000 rifles, 900 sabres, and 16 guns, and that he might be attacked by the combined forces of Jackson and Ewell with a strength of 17,000 and 48 guns.

May 13th.—Banks withdrew with his division, 8,000 strong, from Harrisonburg to Strasburg. Kenly was at Front Royal with 1,000 men.

May 18th.—The opposing troops were now distributed as follows: Johnston had 50,000 men at Richmond, McClellan had 105,000 west of West Point; Anderson, 10,000 strong, faced McDowell north of Fredericksburg with 31,000 men and 100 guns.   Shields had 11,000 at Catlett's Station; Geary had 2,000 south of Rectorytown.   At Winchester and at Harper's Ferry there were 4,500.   Banks had 8,000 at Strasburg, and Kenly had 1,000 at Front Royal.   Frémont's command at Franklin was 17,000 strong.   Jackson had 8,000 at Mount Solon and Ewell had 8,500 at Swift Run Gap.

Ewell rode over to Mount Solon to arrange a plan of operations.   It was agreed that Taylor's Brigade of Ewell's Division should unite with Jackson at Sparta, while the remainder of the division marched down the South Fork of the Shenandoah to Luray.

May 19th.—Jackson advanced and reached Newmarket on May 20th.   Here he was joined by Taylor's Brigade.   Ashby received orders to leave a portion of his force to deceive Banks, and to prevent information reaching him, while he joined Jackson with the remainder of his force.

May 21st.—Jackson reached the vicinity of Luray, joining the remainder of Ewell's Division.

May 23rd.—Jackson, having joined Ewell at Luray, bringing his force up to a total of 16,000 rifles, 1,200 sabres, and 48 guns, advanced up the Luray-Winchester road to Front Royal, where he attacked and defeated a Federal detachment, capturing 600 men and two guns.   Jackson, in advancing to attack the Federals at Front Royal, attempted to surround their forces.   For this purpose, he diverted the cavalry at Spanglers by the road across McCoy's Ford to destroy the railway and telegraph between Front Royal and Strasburg, where Banks' main body was, and thus to prevent reinforcements being sent from there.   Part of Ashby's cavalry was to threaten the Federals' rear, while Jackson, with the main body moving off the main road, was to cut off the Federals from Manassas Gap by approaching Front Royal from the south.   Kenly, the Federal commander, and his force, 1,000 strong, were surprised, as he was without any cavalry.   In order to avoid disaster, he retreated towards Winchester. He was able only partially to destroy the bridge over the North Fork of the Shenandoah.   Jackson pursued with a small force of cavalry and caught up Kenly's troops at Cedarville.   The Federals' retreat now became a rout.   Kenly lost 900 men, of whom 750 were taken prisoner.   These results were due mainly to Ashby's energy and to the excellent handling of his cavalry.

He carried out the rôle in the battle allotted to him by Jackson, and in addition interrupted the railway near Buckton and drove back the Federal guard there.   Of Jackson's infantry and artillery only the advanced guard was engaged. His main body reached Front Royal during the evening.

When Banks realized the disaster to Kenly's command, he considered that Jackson was intending to advance on Winchester, with a view to cutting off his line of retreat and supply.   The courses open to him were (1) to withdraw rapidly to Winchester; (2) to endeavour to attack the Confederates in flank towards Front Royal; (3) to retreat over the Little North Mountains to the River Potomac; (4) to wait for reinforcements from the 17,000 men under Frémont at Franklin.   He decided on the first alternative.   Jackson, being uncertain what Banks would do, advanced to a central point at Middletown, from which place he could move against Strasburg or Winchester or against Banks' flank if he advanced towards Washington.   He sent cavalry towards Strasburg to gain information as to Banks' movements.   The Confederate cavalry gained contact with the enemy's train near Middletown and caused considerable confusion before they were driven back by the Federal infantry.

Banks continued his retreat more rapidly after this incident, so that by the time Jackson's main body reached Middletown the Federal infantry were clear of this place.   Jackson sent forward all available cavalry and supported them with infantry. Unfortunately, after Ashby's cavalry had gained an initial success by driving the Federals off the main road and harassing their retreat, they did not continue to press the retreating enemy, but instead stopped to plunder.   Had the Confederate cavalry maintained their pressure, they might have turned Banks' retreat into a rout.

McClellan continued his advance towards Richmond.

May 24th.—In consequence of this success by Jackson, McClellan was ordered to send Shields' Division to co-operate with Frémont, and McDowell was withdrawn from the main Federal striking force for a third time.   The Federals thus lost an opportunity of capturing Richmond.   McClellan's force might at this time have been raised to 150,000.   Instead of concentrating all available numbers with his main army under McClellan at the decisive point, the President retained troops to prevent Jackson and Anderson marching on the capital.

Jackson continued his march on Winchester.   Ewell advanced from Front Royal to within three miles of Winchester, where he bivouacked.   Banks retreated.   His losses in stores were heavy.

BATTLE OF WINCHESTER.

May 25th.—Jackson's force of seven brigades and 48 guns with Stuart's cavalry attacked, soon after dawn, the Federals, numbering 5,000 rifles, 1,500 sabres, and 16 guns, in position south of Winchester and north of Abraham's Creek. The Stonewall Brigade turned the Federal right flank, while Ewell's brigades attacked their left flank. A Federal counter-attack on their right was repulsed with loss. Jackson pressed forward against the centre and right, gradually extending beyond the Federals' flank.

As soon as the Confederates' flanking movements threatened the Federals' retreat, they withdrew and they were driven back through Winchester. At this place 700 prisoners and £60,000 worth of stores were captured.

There was no pursuit by the cavalry after this battle, as Stuart did not act on his own initiative in the final phase of the battle, but waited for orders, and as Ashby's cavalry were not concentrated after their pillaging expeditions. The Federals' flight northwards by the Martinsburg road was so rapid that the Confederate infantry and artillery could not keep touch with them. Banks halted for a few hours at Martinsburg and then crossed the River Potomac and pushed on to Williamsport during the night. The Confederates went into camp at Stephenson's Depot.

May 28th.—Jackson attacked Saxton, who had advanced from Harper's Ferry. This was in accordance with instructions received to threaten Maryland with invasion and a movement against Washington to draw off as many troops as possible from McDowell and McClellan. Accordingly Winder, with four regiments and two batteries, had been sent towards Charlestown, which was occupied by a detachment sent by Saxton commanding a force of 7,000 Federals at Harper's Ferry.

May 29th.—Jackson took up a position near Halltown. His advanced troops came into contact with the Federals on the Bolivar and Loudon Heights.

Saxton, fearing that he might be cut off if the Confederates crossed the River Potomac above Harper's Ferry, withdrew over the river during the night.

Shields' Division was within striking distance of Front Royal on this day.

Jackson, with a force of 16,000, now found himself threatened by large numbers of the enemy. In his front was Banks with 7,000; Saxton was at Harper's Ferry with 7,000; Frémont was marching with 15,000 via Wardensville towards his rear; Shields was converging with 10,000 via Front Royal.

McDowell also had 20,000 men in the vicinity. Jackson's troops, by rapid marching, passed through Strasburg and escaped from the converging forces.

May 30th.—McDowell, with two divisions, reached Rectortown. Jackson now realized that if he was to elude the Federal forces converging on him he must retire at once on Winchester. He therefore ordered an immediate withdrawal, and reached Winchester before dark, after a twenty-five mile march. His force was now eighteen miles from Strasburg, whereas McDowell's divisions, 30,000 strong, at Front Royal were twelve miles east of this place, and Frémont, commanding a force of 15,000 men, at Wardensville, was eighteen miles west of it. Saxton and Banks, with 14,000 men from the River Potomac, were advancing on him from the north. Altogether, nearly 60,000 Federals were converging on his force, which was approximately a quarter of the numerical strength of the total forces opposed to him.

May 31st.—Jackson's main body reached Strasburg. His rearguard, under Winder, arrived at Newtown. Shields distributed his four brigades on the approaches towards Front Royal, as he was uncertain as to Jackson's strength, and he thought that Longstreet's Division was advancing up the Luray road to reinforce him. Frémont reached Cedar Creek. Saxton was at Charlestown.

June 1st.—On this day General Jackson marched through Winchester to Strasburg, in order to escape from the combined forces of Shields and Frémont, who were marching on this place. Jackson's force was completely clear of Strasburg by the time the forces of Frémont and Shields effected a junction. On this day his force marched twenty-eight miles.

Jackson sent some of his cavalry to burn the White House and Columbia Bridges and so to prevent the Federal troops crossing by the roads leading to Newmarket, in order to join Frémont.

McDowell ordered Shields to march towards Strasburg. Shields, however, advanced on Winchester, and thus all chance was lost of intercepting his march in a southerly direction. Shields was then instructed to march down the Luray Valley.

June 2nd.—Jackson, continuing to withdraw up the Shenandoah Valley, reached Mount Jackson, followed by Frémont. Frémont and Shields followed up by the Staunton-Winchester road and the Luray-Front Royal road respectively. They were thus separated by the Massanuttons and by the South Fork River.

June 3rd.—Confederates reached Newmarket.

June 5th.—Jackson reached Harrisonburg and then left the main road and turned in a south-easterly direction towards Port Republic. Through Brown's Gap, five miles south-east of Port Republic, there was the most direct route on to the Virginia Central Railway. He established a signal station south of the Massanuttons, so that he could receive information as to the Federals advancing down on either side of these mountains. He evacuated his casualties to Staunton. He had the bridge at Conrad's Store destroyed, in order to delay the possible junction of Federal troops by the Harrisonburg-Gordonsville road.

He held the bridge at Port Republic, where the Confederates rested until June 8th. He sent his prisoners to the railway at Waynesboro, and parked his trains at Port Republic. Ewell's Division was sent to Cross Keys, and Winder's Brigade was posted on the heights commanding the approaches by which Shields could reach Port Republic.

June 6th.—Ashby, who had been covering Jackson's retreat down the main road, was killed near Harrisonburg.

In the preceding thirty-five days, Jackson's force had marched 245 miles and had won four battles.

BATTLE OF CROSS KEYS.

June 8th.—Battle of Cross Keys was fought by General Ewell, while Jackson contained Shields at Port Republic. Jackson was on interior lines between the two Federal forces advancing up the Valley, and had planned to strike Shields while holding off Frémont. The Confederate forces consisted of Jackson's Division commanded by Winder as senior Brigadier, who had his own brigade and also Patton's and Taliaferro's. Ewell's Division consisted of four brigades, under Trimble, Elzey, G. H. Steuart, and Taylor. The Federal forces consisted of three divisions. Frémont commanded Blenker's Division consisting of Stahl's, Bohlen's and Steinwehr's Brigades, and also Milroy's Division, consisting of Schenck's and Cluseret's Brigades. Shields' Division had two brigades, namely, Tyler's and Carroll's. Frémont, with 12,000 men, advanced against Ewell at Cross Keys, and at the same time Shields' advanced troops entered Port Republic.

Jackson drove back Shields' advanced troops, with a loss to them of 40 men and 2 guns, over the South river and secured Port Republic. To guard against further attacks, Taliaferro's Brigade was left in Port Republic and the Stonewall Brigade was left opposite Lewiston. The third brigade of Winder's Division was held in reserve to help Ewell. Ewell at the same time was able to deal with Frémont's

attacks.   Ewell's troops occupied a wooded ridge through
the centre of which ran the road from Brown's Gap to
Harrisonburg.   The Federal position was on an opposite
ridge.   The Confederates held their position with two brigades
as forward troops, with one brigade in reserve; and their
artillery behind the centre of their front line.

Frémont made use of five brigades in his initial operations,
namely, two brigades against the Confederates' right, held by
Trimble's Brigade, two brigades against the centre of the
Confederates' position, held by Trimble's left and Steuart's
right, and one brigade against Steuart's left flank.

The Confederate commander kept Elzey's Brigade in reserve.
The Federal artillery was located opposite the positions occupied by the Confederates' artillery.   In the first attack made
by the Federals, Trimble's Brigade repulsed Stahl's Brigade.

Ewell at once followed up this success by reinforcing where
his troops had been successful with two regiments from
Elzey's reserve brigade.   Trimble's reinforced brigade
advanced and enveloped the Federals' left flank.

Milroy's Brigade attacking against the Confederates' centre
was also repulsed.   The Federals did not co-ordinate their
attacks to make them simultaneous against the whole position
occupied by the Confederates.

After the attack of Milroy's Brigade had been checked,
Schenck's Brigade attacked the Confederates' left flank.
Ewell now brought up reinforcements to held Schenck's
Brigade, while the advance on his right flank was affecting
Frémont's plan.   The defeat of his left and centre caused
the Federal commander to withdraw Schenck's Brigade in
conformity with a general retreat on his whole front.

During this battle at Cross Keys, Shields was inactive at
Port Republic.

BATTLE OF PORT REPUBLIC.

June 9th.—Jackson's plan was to contain Frémont with
Trimble's and part of Patton's Brigades while he attacked and
drove back Shields' troops from the vicinity of Port Republic
and Lewiston with the remainder of his force.   He then
intended to bring all his available strength to bear against
Frémont's force and to drive him back from Cross Keys and
away from Shields.   The Federals' advanced position, covering Lewiston, held by 2,500 men, with 1,500 in support, was
a strong one on a frontage of about two miles.   Jackson was
acting on interior lines at these battles on June 8th and 9th
against his two opponents, but he had too little space between
his two battlefields at Cross Keys and Port Republic to be

able to disregard the one and use his whole force against the other.

Jackson at first attacked in insufficient strength, with one brigade against Tyler holding a strong position with eight battalions, 16 guns, and a detachment of cavalry. This attack was made against the right flank of the Federals, and was defeated with loss. Jackson then attacked through the woods south of Lewiston. This was successful, and caused the Federal commander—General Tyler—to recall the troops that were pressing forward on his right.

This led to confusion. Jackson then made a general advance and drove the whole Federal force north up the Luray-Front Royal road. When the Federals retreated Jackson retired up the Valley to Brown's Gap, where he was in communication with Richmond, and where he had an almost impregnable defensive position. To have followed up the Federals would have taken him too far from Lee's army at Richmond.

In the fighting on these two days, the Confederates lost 804 men and the Federals had 1,000 casualties and 8 guns. In this Valley campaign, though Jackson's force was never more than 17,000, he had to deal with forces three times as numerous. And yet he was, except at Cross Keys, in superior numbers during engagements with the Federals, who for this reason always exaggerated his numbers.

Frémont and Shields should have joined forces at Winchester. McDowell should not have sent Shields forward alone. He should have supported him with another division.

By marching on either side of the Massanutton Mountains, they could not combine against Jackson until they reached their southern end. Then Jackson had the opportunity of striking them separately. His success was largely due to the rapidity of his marching, to his skilful use of the Massanuttons parallel to the lines of operation, and to the fact that the Federals, though superior in numbers, if united, did not bring their total forces together at the decisive time and place.

In this action the dangers of divided command are apparent. Frémont and Shields did not know each other's movements, and consequently there was indecision by both commanders. They were on exterior lines, and, united, might have had 25,000 men to oppose to Jackson's 13,000. The country, however, was admirably suited to operations on interior lines, and Jackson made full use of the mobility of his troops. Frémont, with superior numbers at Cross Keys, handled his command weakly, whereas in this battle, Ewell showed excellent judgment in reserving the fire of his troops till the enemy were within sixty paces, in delivering a counter-stroke on the

Federal left, and in his judicious refusal to pursue as night was coming on. Pursuit was not in accordance with Jackson's general plan. At the same time, Jackson saved his command by acting promptly and vigorously at Port Republic. At this battle, the Federal General Tyler held a well-chosen position with skill and determination. His defeat was brought about by the turning movement directed by Jackson and carried out with great courage by his Louisiana troops.

Jackson's losses, however, were heavy, owing to his hurried attack against Shields whom he hoped to defeat in the morning so that he could turn to attack Frémont in the afternoon.

June 12th.—Jackson's force was in the vicinity of Weyer's Cave, where he remained till June 17th.

June 17th.—Jackson began to march towards Richmond, and thus the Shenandoah Valley campaign was terminated.

In " Jackson's Valley Campaign," Allan writes as follows :

" The operations of General Jackson in the Valley during 1862 constitute one of the most brilliant episodes of the great Civil War. The theatre on which they took place afforded a quick and easy approach to the Federal capital. The mountains and rivers of the Valley gave to an active and skilful commander many opportunities of neutralizing great disparity of force. This campaign had a most important bearing on all the military operations in Virginia, for he checked forces four or five times as numerous as his own, and thus paralysed McClellan. It is an admirable example of an aggressive-defensive campaign."

CHAPTER III.

PRINCIPLES OF WAR ILLUSTRATED.

I.—MAINTENANCE OF THE AIM IN WAR.

(a) All Jackson's operations in the Shenandoah Valley were carried out for the purpose of containing as many Federals as possible there and thus preventing them from augmenting their main army. He maintained his objective when he brought on the Battle of Kernstown on March 23rd, 1862, in spite of the fact that he was outnumbered by 3,600 infantry and 460 sabres.

Although he was defeated tactically and forced to withdraw, he alarmed Lincoln for the safety of Washington.

The President then further disseminated his forces by detaching McDowell from McClellan's army, by effectually preventing combined operations by making independent commands—i.e., McClellan to command the troops in the Yorktown Peninsula, Frémont to command in West Virginia, Banks to command the Shenandoah Valley troops, McDowell to command the Rappahannock Corps. Also the President recalled Williams' Division to Winchester, and Blenker's Division was sent to West Virginia.

Jackson continued to maintain his objective by occupying a position at Rude's Hill south of Mount Jackson, where he checked and contained Banks' two divisions, and thus prevented them from helping McClellan.

(b) Jackson continued to maintain his objective in the Valley though his force was only 6,000 and Banks had a force, 20,000 strong, of two divisions under Shields and Williams.

On April 19th, 1862, he reached Swift Run Gap, where he was on the flank of Banks' advance on Staunton. He was able to transfer his base to Gordonsville and to gain touch with Ewell's force of 8,500 men.

Ewell's and Johnson's troops west of Staunton were placed under Jackson's command on April 29th.

In order to prevent troops from being transferred to Yorktown to oppose Johnson and Magruder there, Jackson left Ewell's troops in Swift Run Gap while with his force he marched up the Shenandoah river to Port Republic; then he

38

turned east to cross the Blue Ridge at Brown's Gap; then he marched south to Mechum's Station.

On hearing of this movement, President Lincoln again failed to maintain his objective.

He became alarmed for the safety of the capital and halted McDowell at Fredericksburg, and transferred Shields' Division from Harrisonburg to reinforce McDowell.

Jackson continued to engage Banks' attention by marching from Mechum's to Staunton. He then marched north-west towards McDowell village, where, after joining forces with Johnson, he attacked the advanced guard of Frémont's Division and drove them back.

He then created a further diversion in favour of his main field army. He called up half Ewell's force from Swift Run Gap and marched via Harrisonburg on to Newmarket, while the remainder of Ewell's force marched north on the east side of the Massanuttons.

At Newmarket, Jackson turned north-east to join Ewell at Luray. The march was then continued in a northerly direction to Front Royal. Here Jackson attacked a detachment sent by Banks from Strasburg. This detachment was completely defeated, and the railway between Front Royal and Strasburg was cut.

Banks then withdrew to Winchester. Jackson followed up by the main road from Strasburg, while Ewell advanced direct on to Winchester from Front Royal. On May 25th, Jackson attacked Banks at Winchester, and drove his force out of the town towards the River Potomac.

This victory caused Lincoln again to fail in maintaining his objective. McDowell was withheld from McClellan.

Shields' Division was sent to help Frémont to intercept Jackson.

These orders completely upset McClellan's plans and reduced his chances of capturing Richmond.

Jackson continued to keep the Federals' attention occupied. He now advanced towards Harper's Ferry, and thus contained 25,000 under Frémont and Shields, 7,000 under Banks, 7,000 under Saxton, 20,000 under McDowell.

In order to avoid the converging movements of Frémont and Shields, Jackson now counter-marched south. He passed through Strasburg on June 1st before his pursuers reached this place.

The two Federal Generals continued the pursuit in a southerly direction. Jackson then planned to defeat the enemy in detail by containing Frémont while he defeated Shields, then he proposed to cross the South River and attack Frémont while he held off Shields.

On June 8th, however, Frémont attacked Ewell at Cross Keys and was defeated.

On June 9th, in the Battle of Port Republic, Jackson forced Shields to retire north towards Luray.

The result of these successes was that McDowell again was stopped from joining McClellan.   Lincoln again failed to maintain his objective.

This was particularly unfortunate for the commander in the field, as his army was in an unfavourable position astride the River Chickahominy, with his right flank on the York river, in order to co-operate with McDowell, whom he was expecting to advance from the north.   This unfavourable position was the result of Jackson's operations.

(c) The whole of Jackson's plans were upset by civilian interference at the beginning of 1862.   The objective for his operations was to secure a fertile district from which to draw supplies; to obtain a base for operations against the Federals in Western Virginia, and to be astride their communications between Fredericksburg and Western Virginia.

In addition to gaining these objectives, Jackson placed his opponents on the defensive.

For these operations at this time he had 10,000 rifles, 600 sabres under Ashby, and five batteries.

On New Year's Day he took the offensive against Kelly, in order to obtain his first objectives—namely, Bath and Hancock.   With these in his possession he would cut the communications between Rosecrans and Banks, and he would isolate the Romney garrison.

Bath, with a large quantity of stores, was captured on January 4th.   On the following day, the Cacepon Canal dam was destroyed, Hancock was bombarded, and the railway and telegraph south of the River Potomac in the vicinity of Bath and Hancock were cut.

By January 14th, he reached, after very arduous marches in bitter weather, Romney, which on the 10th had been abandoned by Kelly.   Here he captured much stores, equipment, and ammunition.

Jackson now left Loring in command of this place.   All this work and effort were rendered useless by the Confederate Secretary of State for War ordering Jackson to recall Loring.

Jackson, now at Winchester, was with 4,600 men exposed to attacks from Shields, who reoccupied Romney on February 7th, and from Banks north of the River Potomac.

Jackson, as a protest, sent in his resignation.   Luckily for the Confederate cause, this was later withdrawn.

II.—ECONOMY OF FORCE.

(a) Jackson's operations for three months in the Shenandoah Valley caused the Federals to dissipate their forces.

By his secret and rapid marches he neutralized the disparity between his own force and his enemies. He wrecked McClellan's Yorktown campaign and contained forces four times as strong as his own. Even when he suffered a tactical reverse at Kernstown he caused the Federal President to recall Banks' troops and to suspend the movement of McDowell's detachment.

Even when he had drawn upon his force of 16,000 men the attentions of 60,000 Federals, who were trying to combine in order to crush him, he not only eluded them by a rapid retirement up the Valley, but he then defeated Frémont and Shields at Cross Keys and Port Republic.

Owing to the operations of the Valley detachment under Jackson, McDowell was in all five times withdrawn from McClellan. Jackson, therefore, skilfully showed the proper use of a detachment, as he assisted his main army at Richmond, and contained larger numbers of the Federals than his own force.

(b) Jackson's action at Kernstown, March 23rd, 1862, caused the Federal President to dissipate his forces. He became alarmed for the safety of Washington. He brought Williams' divisions to Winchester. Blenker's Division was sent to join Frémont in West Virginia. McDowell's Corps, 40,000 strong, was halted at Manassas.

(c) The plan of campaign adopted by the Federals in 1862 caused a dissipation of their forces. The plan was to move their main army by sea to Fort Monroe and then west up the Yorktown Peninsula to Richmond.

When McClellan landed with his army of 58,000 and 100 guns at this place on April 2nd, he was 130 miles away from Washington, which could be threatened by troops in the Shenandoah Valley. Therefore, the President rightly insisted on having the capital, as it was the base and seat of government, adequately secured. For this he settled that a detachment of 55,000 would be required.

To avoid this considerable dissipation of force, McClellan might have made a direct advance via Centreville and Manassas on Richmond. This would have covered the capital, as on the way he would have had to deal with Johnston's main army at Centreville.

This course would have satisfied the President, and would thus have economized men, as it could have reduced the actual detachments necessary for the local protection of Washington, and for dealing with the Confederates' Shenandoah Valley army.

McClellan did not in this case make the Confederates' main army his objective, but aimed his blow at their capital.

The other plans which he proposed similarly left Washington uncovered by his main army.   His alternatives were to make use of sea power and to disembark his army either at Acquia Creek at the mouth of the Rappahannock, at the mouth of the York River, or at Fort Monroe.

In none of these schemes were his direct land communications with Washington safeguarded, and the Confederates in the Valley were a constant menace to them and to the capital.

Therefore, whenever a diversion was made in this quarter by Jackson, the President prevented McClellan from economizing his forces.   The reason for the adoption of the plan of taking the main Federal Army to Fort Monroe was that, by advancing in a westerly direction on the capital from this place, the flanks would be secured by the York and James rivers.

However, all the time that McClellan's army was on the water and until he was actively engaging the Confederates, their capital could be assailed by superior forces.   McClellan's army was reduced by 73,000 men with troops left at Warrenton, at Manassas, in the Shenandoah Valley, in West Virginia, and in the thirty-three-mile cordon of forts round Washington from Alexandria beyond the Arlington Heights to Chain Bridge and Bladensburg.

The drawback to the Monroe plan was that it necessitated an advance through unknown country, and McClellan, who was naturally cautious, advanced very slowly.   Also the Confederates had their ship *Merrimac* in the James river and batteries at Norfolk, Gloucester, and Yorktown.

Had McClellan adopted a direct advance on Richmond by land, he would have satisfied the President, he would have covered his communications, and he would have economized his forces.

(*d*) At the Battle of First Bull Run on July 21st, 1861, the Federals dissipated their forces.   McDowell turned Beauregard's northern flank with two divisions, while part of one division advanced in the centre by Stone Bridge.

The remainder of his force covered the communications with Alexandria.   One of these divisions was at Centreville.

The result was that, as McDowell did not pin the Confederates to their ground on their six miles of front, they were able to reinforce their left flank when the Federal divisions crossed the river at Sudley and Red House Fords in their turning movement.

McDowell did not make use of his superiority of 7,000 infantry to make a concerted attack with all available force, and the result was that he was defeated.

(e) General Patterson's detachment of 14,000 Federals was not an economy of force, as it did not carry out the rôle of a detachment in containing the Confederates opposed to him at the Battle of First Bull Run.

When Beauregard held Manassas Junction with 20,000 men faced by five Federal divisions under McDowell, Johnston, by demonstrations, contained Patterson in the Valley and then slipped away via Ashby's Gap to join Beauregard. His four brigades, 22 guns, and cavalry were a valuable addition to the Confederate General, as they arrived in time for the battle on July 21st.

Patterson had superior numbers, and he should have justified the existence of his detachment either by attacking the Confederates and driving them up the Valley, or at least by taking up a position to prevent the junction of the Army of the Shenandoah with the six brigades of the Army of the Potomac.

He did neither of these things, and when he found that he was no longer in touch with Johnston he retired, on July 18th, to Harper's Ferry. His detachment was, therefore, ineffective.

III.—SURPRISE.

(a) Jackson in the Shenandoah Valley was always endeavouring to outwit his adversary. In spite of the fact that his total forces were inferior to the Federals opposed to him, and that his troops were often short of ammunition and without boots and equipment, he was eminently successful in his operations and in creating alarm at Washington.

Between May 5th and June 7th, Jackson fought and won four important battles and marched 245 miles.

His unexpected appearance at Kernstown, his withdrawal to Swift Run Gap, his junction with Johnson near Staunton, his engagement against Milroy at McDowell, his counter-march and unexpected appearance and successes at Front Royal and at Winchester, his retirement up the Valley, and his defeat of Frémont at Cross Keys and Shields at Port Republic led to important far-reaching results.

He considerably delayed the end of the campaign by his manœuvres and weakened the Federal field army at the decisive point.

Lee also endeavoured to gain the advantage of surprise as often as possible. His achievements in effecting a junction of his forces on the battlefield at Gaines' Mill, at Groveton, at Fredericksburg, and at Chancellorsville enabled him to surprise the Federals on each of these occasions.

(b) On May 23rd, 1862, Colonel Kenly, with a detachment of 1,000 men and two guns, was completely surprised at Front Royal by Jackson's Brigade. He had no protective detachments watching the possible approaches to his position in the Luray Valley.

The Confederate infantry attacked in front while Flournoy, with 250 sabres, attacked his right flank. The Federals retreated up the Winchester road.

As they approached Cedarville, Kenly tried to rally and check the advance of the Confederates. They were again surprised by a charge of four squadrons under Fleurnoy, who captured 600 men and 2 guns.

Banks, at Strasburg, was also completely surprised by Jackson's action to Front Royal. It was not until 10 a.m. on the following day that he would believe that Jackson's force had been attacking. He thought that Jackson was still on the main Valley road west of the Massanuttons.

He then had to decide hurriedly whether he would remain at Strasburg and wait for Frémont, who was now at Franklin to reinforce him there, or to escape to Manassas by attacking and driving away Jackson's force at Front Royal, or to retire on Winchester.

He chose the latter course.

Had it not been that Jackson's men were tired after their recent efforts, that Ashby's cavalry discontinued their pursuit as they scattered in order to pillage, and that the Federals made a rapid march, the result of the surprise to Banks and his consequent hurried retreat might have been disastrous.

As it was, they had time to organize their retreat between Newtown and Winchester and to delay Jackson's advance in a series of strong rearguard positions.

(c) Jackson's movements leading up to the Battle of McDowell Village on May 8th, 1862, mystified and misled Banks, alarmed the Federal President, and led to the defeat of the advanced troops of Milroy and Schenck.

At the end of April, Lee had told Jackson that the Federals were in force at Fredericksburg, and that it would be a suitable time to strike suddenly against Federal detachments in his neighbourhood, as these would have to be weakened in order to add to the numbers at Fredericksburg, who were opposed only by Anderson's force of 12,000 men. The Federals at this place were 33,000 strong.

At this time, Ewell, with 8,500 men, was at Standardsville,

E. Johnson's Brigade of 2,800 men, 3 batteries, and some cavalry, was at Staunton, and Jackson was at Swift Run Gap.

The troops with which Jackson would have to deal were Banks' at Harrisonburg, Frémont's at Franklin with his advanced troops, 6,800 strong, in front of E. Johnson.

In order to relieve the situation at Fredericksburg and at Yorktown at this time, where McClellan had more than twice as many troops as the Confederates, the following courses were open to Jackson:—

For Jackson and Ewell to combine, bringing their strength up to 16,500, and operate against Banks by advancing either up to Front Royal or to Luray, and then marching south to take him in the rear.

This would have isolated E. Johnson's Brigade at Staunton, and would have enabled Milroy and Schenck to bring superior forces to bear against it.   It was decided, therefore, to leave Ewell in Swift Run Gap to contain Banks twenty-nine miles west of his position at this Gap, while Jackson joined E. Johnson and attacked the leading Federal brigade under Milroy, 3,300 strong, at McDowell.

There was a better chance of effecting a surprise and of gaining a victory, as Milroy was detached from Schenck, who was at Franklin.   Banks' force was more concentrated than Frémont's.   Also between the two parts of the Valley in this latter case the distance would only be fifty-four miles, whereas if Jackson and Ewell marched north to Manassas Gap they would then be eighty miles from E. Johnson and fifty-four miles from Banks.

Jackson, therefore, marched from Swift Run on April 30th up the South Fork River to Port Republic, then in an easterly direction through Brown's Gap to Mechum's Station, and there he entrained his force and reached Staunton by rail by May 5th.

Banks on this day retired up the Turnpike road to New-market.   Jackson chose this circuitous route in order to mystify his opponents while Ashby was making demonstrations towards Harrisonburg.   He then marched west and joined E. Johnson and was able to bring superior numbers to bear against the Federal commanders, who were defeated and forced to retire on Franklin.

(d) At the Battle of Bull Run on July 21st, 1861, McDowell advanced his centre and sent his right wing, consisting of two divisions, round the Confederates' left flank.   These divisions, owing to the wooded nature of the country, had been able to concentrate on the north bank opposite the fords unobserved.   The bulk of the Confederates were on their right flank.

The Federals at first gained an advantage until Jackson's Brigade made a strong resistance at Henry House Hill.

The Federals then were completely surprised by an attack on their southern flank by Kirby Smith's Brigade of 1,900 fresh troops, which had detrained at Manassas Junction, four miles from the place where they came into action between Newmarket and Bald Hill.   Beauregard took advantage of this surprise attack to order a general advance, and the result was that the Federals were completely routed.

(e) General Johnston surprised Patterson by slipping away from the Valley to join Beauregard in time for the First Bull Run battle when it was essential for him to prevent Johnston from reinforcing the main Confederate army opposing McDowell's five divisions.

(f) At the Battle of First Bull Run, July 21st, 1861, there was a series of surprises.

In the first place, Patterson, who had 14,000 Federals with which to deal with General Johnston's 10,000 Confederates, allowed Johnston to escape from the Valley in time to take part in the battle on July 21st.

During the fighting on this day, the Confederates were surprised by the advance of two Federal divisions south of the River Bull Run against their left flank at a time when the bulk of their force was on the right.

Jackson's Brigade saved the situation by coming up at the critical moment to a position, which they held on Henry House Hill.   Here they checked the advance of McDowell's divisions. There was heavy fighting round this position, where the Federals had a great superiority in numbers.

The issue was finally decided by the arrival of a fresh brigade, 1,900 strong, under Kirby Smith.   These troops detrained at Manassas Junction and marched against the southern flank of the Federals attacking the Stonewall Brigade.

The result was a complete surprise for the Federal right, which withdrew.   After a short resistance, their retreat, followed up by Confederate cavalry, became a rout.   Had the pursuit been continued on the following days, Washington might have been captured.

IV.—MOBILITY.

(a) Jackson's mobility in his Valley campaign of 1862 was most effective by enabling him either to strike the Federals or to escape from them.

After the Battle of Kernstown on March 23rd, 1862, owing to his tactical defeat he was forced to withdraw.   On the 25th he reached Mount Jackson, twenty-five miles from Banks' position at Strasburg.   In order to fight the Battle of Kernstown, Jackson marched thirty-six miles in two days.

Jackson's activity and mobility during May greatly helped the Confederates' main army in front of Richmond in containing superior numbers of the enemy and in causing diversions of Federal troops from McClellan's army.

By May 3rd, with a force of 6,000 men, he had reached Mechum's River Station, having left Swift Run on the afternoon of April 30th.   By May 5th he had joined E. Johnson's Brigade at Staunton.

On May 7th he marched west and fought Milroy and Schenck on the following day at the Battle of McDowell. His force had now covered seventy-five miles.

On May 9th he pursued the Federals and reached Franklin on the 11th.   He was then obliged to withdraw owing to the proximity of Frémont and Banks.   By the 15th his force was at Lebanon Springs.

Five days later he had reached Newmarket, having marched a further eighty miles via Mount Solon, Harrison, and Sparta. He then crossed the Massanuttons into the Luray Valley on May 21st, where he joined Ewell, and continued his march towards Front Royal, where on the 23rd he attacked and defeated Kenly's detachment.

On the 25th he was twenty-five miles farther north.   On this day he defeated Banks at Winchester and pursued him up to Harper's Ferry.

On May 29th he realized that Federal troops were converging on to his force from the east and west.   In order to escape, he had to march back through Winchester, and he was able to be clear of Strasburg by the time that Frémont and Shields reached this place.   Jackson then withdrew, destroying the bridges on the Newmarket-Luray road.

On June 2nd he reached Mount Jackson and on the 3rd he was at Newmarket, where he destroyed the bridge over the North Fork river.

On the 5th he reached Harrisonburg and on the following day he was in a position at Port Republic commanding the routes by which Frémont and Shields could meet south of the Massanuttons.

Though the forces under both Frémont and Shields marched well, they were unable to intercept Jackson in his march to Port Republic.   Frémont's force covered eighty miles from Franklin to Strasburg in six days.   Shields marched from Fredericksburg to Front Royal, a distance of eighty miles, in five and a half days. Jackson, owing to his mobility, having eluded his two opponents and prevented their junction by burning the bridges across the River Shenandoah below Port Republic, was able to make further use of the mobility of his force by fighting them in detail.

On June 8th, at Cross Keys, Ewell, with 6,000 men, dealt with Frémont's attack and drove his troops back.

On the following day he contained Frémont and defeated Shields in the Battle of Port Republic.

Thus, owing to his mobility, Jackson, with 13,000 men, was able to defeat 25,000 Federals.

On June 17th he started on his march to Richmond via Gordonsville. He arrived at Ashland Station on June 25th. On June 27th he was co-operating in the Battle of Gaines' Mill against McClellan's right flank, east of Richmond, over a hundred miles from Port Republic.

(b) After the Battle of McDowell Village on May 8th, 1862, in which Milroy's attempt to capture the Federal position on Sitlington Hill was unsuccessful, had Jackson made use of the mobility of his cavalry supported by infantry he might have turned the Federal retreat into a rout. But there was no immediate pursuit, so that Milroy and Schenck were able to fall back unmolested on Frémont at Franklin, covered by forest fires which they had made.

(c) At the Battle of First Bull Run on July 21st, 1861, the Confederates added to their mobility by the use of the railway. Johnston entrained his infantry at Piedmont on the Manassas Gap Railway on July 19th, when he learnt that McDowell was advancing on Manassas against Beauregard with 35,000 men in five divisions.

The cavalry, after demonstrating against Patterson in order to prevent him from finding out about the movements of the Shenandoah Army, joined the artillery and train and marched to Beauregard. Luckily for the Confederates McDowell did not attack on the 19th and 20th.

By the next day, Beauregard's force numbered 28,000, including 2,500 cavalry and 29 guns. Kirby Smith's Brigade detrained on the field while the battle was in progress, in time to deliver a final and decisive blow against the Federals' right flank.

(d) The charge by Jackson's cavalry at Cedarville is an excellent example of the effect that may be produced by a combination of mobility and determination. A small force of horsemen successfully dispersed their opponents by riding right into their ranks. The mobility of Jackson's horsemen was of inestimable advantage throughout this Valley campaign.   The Confederates had information while the Federals were usually without it.   Kenly at Front Royal was completely surprised on May 23rd, as he had no cavalry.   Jackson made full use of the mobility of his mounted troops by keeping them well out to his front to obtain information and to form a screen which the Federals could not penetrate.   Consequently, the work for infantry with advanced and flank guards was considerably lightened.

V.—CO-OPERATION.

(*a*) There was a lack of mobility on the part of the Federals when, after the Battle of Winchester, they failed to intercept Jackson, who, on May 29th, was in the vicinity of Harper's Ferry.   His force of 16,000 men had to escort 2,000 prisoners and their ammunition, supplies, and baggage.   His column was seven miles long.

Yet, though the Stonewall Brigade was forty-three miles from Strasburg, Shields' force was twelve miles and Frémont's troops were twenty miles from this place, there was so little co-operation between the Federal troops that Jackson passed through Strasburg with his whole column and convoy intact.

(*b*) Before the Battle of Front Royal on May 23rd, 1862, there was complete co-operation between Ashby's cavalry operating in front of Banks down the Turnpike road and Jackson's main force east of the Massanuttons on the Luray-Front Royal road.   On the night of May 22nd/23rd, Ashby left only patrols to watch Banks and joined the main column.

One of his regiments was then sent to destroy the railway bridges east of Front Royal and to hold the road to Manassas Gap, while the rest of the cavalry cut the communications between Kenly's troops at Front Royal and the main body at Strasburg.

When Jackson's troops, having advanced through the woods south of Front Royal, attacked the Federal detachment, Ashby's cavalry was on Kenly's right rear.   This caused Kenly to order a retreat.   He was followed up by the infantry. Three miles farther back he tried to re-form, when again the cavalry co-operated by charging.   They captured 600 prisoners and two guns, and the Federals were forced to continue their retreat.

VI.—CONCENTRATION.

(*a*) On June 8th and 9th, 1862, at the Battles of Cross Keys and Port Republic, there was a lack of concentration on the part of the Federals. Jackson had, by June 7th, retired to Port Republic, where, with 6,000 men, he held positions on the heights north of this town and west of the South Fork river to oppose Shields. He left Ewell with 6,000 men at Cross Keys to deal with Frémont.

The Federals in this area had 25,000 men, but they did not keep touch during their pursuit of Jackson's force, and they were ignorant of one another's movements during the fighting on June 8th and 9th.

McDowell did not make use of his superiority in numbers during the pursuit of Jackson's force. He sent Shields' Division on alone. He could have ensured numerical superiority by supporting Shields with Ord's and King's Divisions. Instead he kept these two divisions at Front Royal. This place could have been held by Saxton and Banks while McDowell's whole force pursued Jackson. In this Valley campaign, although the Federals had superior numbers, they were not able to concentrate them at the decisive times and places.

During their march they were divided by the Massanuttons, and during the battles their forces were separated by the South Fork river, as the only bridge was at Port Republic, which was in Jackson's possession.

The topography of the area of operations was certainly in Jackson's favour, and helped his operations on interior lines, but, had there been intercommunication between Shields and Frémont, they might have concentrated south of the Massanuttons and thus would have escaped defeat in detail by a force only a little more than half their total number.

(b) Before the campaign of 1862 started, the Army of Northern Virginia, 47,000 strong, was at Centreville. The Federal commander could have opposed the Confederate commander with 215,000. Had McClellan realized that the Confederates' main army was his objective, and also the anxiety which the President and people felt for their capital, he would have concentrated his forces and advanced direct on Centreville, detaching a proportion of his large force to contain the troops operating in the Shenandoah Valley.

Instead of this concentration of force, troops were left to protect Washington and to garrison the city. Troops were also sent to Yorktown Peninsula by sea.

This movement uncovered the Federal capital, and necessitated, in the opinion of the President, a considerable force for its protection.

This overwhelming numerical superiority which the Federals had at their disposal was not concentrated, with the result that the Confederates, in spite of their limited resources and small man power in comparison with the Northern States, were able to continue the war for four years.

VII.—SECURITY.

(a) Jackson adequately secured his retreat when, on May 29th, 1862, he learnt of the converging movements of Frémont, who pursued him down the Turnpike road, and of Shields, who advanced against him by the Luray-Front Royal road. .

Luckily for Jackson these two forces were separated by the Massanutton Mountains as they marched south.

Jackson further added to his security by breaking the bridges of White House, Columbia, and Conrad's Store, and by holding the remaining bridge of Port Republic with cavalry. Had these precautions not been taken, and had these two Generals carried out McDowell's orders of attacking his flanks and rear simultaneously, their superiority of numbers might have gained a decisive result.

(b) The whole basis of the 1862 campaign was dependent on the security of Washington. President Lincoln approved of McClellan's plan to capture the Confederate capital by marching on it from Fort Monroe up the Yorktown Peninsula on the condition that Washington and Manassas Junction were secure.

McClellan considered that he had fulfilled the conditions by leaving 18,000 men to hold the works on a circumference of thirty-three miles from south of Alexandria round to the River Potomac east of this town.

In addition he left troops at Warrenton, Manassas, and in the Shenandoah Valley. The Federal President did not, however, consider that Washington was adequately secured. It was for this reason that he was particularly sensitive to any threat at his capital, and that McDowell with his force of 40,000 men was five times prevented from joining McClellan east of Richmond—namely, after the Battle of Kernstown, after Jackson's march to Mechum's Station, after the Battle of Winchester, after the Battle of Port Republic, and during Jackson's advance on Richmond via Gordonsville.

Lincoln considered that the best plan would have been to march south against the Confederate capital, so as to cover and secure the capital.

McClellan, however, considered that the state of the roads would make their rate of marching very slow, and that they would depend on a long line of railway, which in the Confederates' country would be particularly liable to raids.

Alternative plans were to embark for Acquia Creek and then to march on Richmond via Fredericksburg.

This would make the marching distance forty miles shorter than in the previous plan.

Another plan would be to move to Urbanna on the south bank of the River Rappahannock, so that the distance by land would be fifty miles, and less than by any other proposed route.

The disadvantage was that two rivers would have to be crossed before Richmond could be reached, and that Urbanna was not a suitable landing place for large bodies of troops. The plan adopted had, however, many disadvantages.

The country between Fort Monroe and Richmond was not known to McClellan, the Confederate vessel, the *Merrimac*, held the James river, and while McClellan's force was in transports on the way to the Yorktown Peninsula Johnston, with a large force from Centreville, might attack and capture Washington.

McClellan did not sufficiently realize how sensitive the President was as to the security of the Federal capital.   It was on this point of security that the campaign against Richmond depended.

McClellan waited for the reinforcements that he hoped would arrive on his right flank, thus giving the Confederates valuable time in which to strengthen their positions; he separated his force by the River Chickahominy, and he had his first base in an exposed position.   He could with 150,000 men, nearly twice as many as the Confederates could collect to meet his advance, have marched on Richmond, leaving 90,000 men to garrison Washington and to hold the northern end of Shenandoah Valley and Manassas Junction.

Therefore, his first plan of a direct advance on land on Richmond could have been carried out more quickly, more easily, and more securely than by any other suggested scheme.

(c) Banks did not, after the Battle of Kernstown, carry out the principles of security as advocated in our Field Service Regulations. He moved very slowly after Jackson, and halted for six days at Strasburg and at Woodstock for six days till April 16th.   He should have tried to catch up Jackson's force and to defeat it as soon as possible after Kernstown.

His cavalry should have followed up the Confederates and should have ascertained their true numbers instead of relying on false reports as to their reinforcements and as to their intention to send Longstreet's Division to help Jackson in an offensive operation against him.

Had he moved at once to Newmarket he would have been

in a secure strategical position, and by sending a detachment to Luray he could have watched Thornton's Gap and Fisher's Gap through which reinforcements might arrive for Jackson. Actually he did not advance until the end of April.   One reason for his slowness was that his administrative arrangements were defective.

His supply trains were deficient and had been ordered to Manassas Junction before the Battle of Kernstown.   They were thus separated from him by sixty miles of road at a time when the weather was bad.

Jackson, on the other hand, did carry out the principles of security.   He rightly withdrew by the North Fork, as, if Banks followed up, it would separate him farther from other Federal troops who might be able to co-operate.   Jackson thought that Banks would endeavour to interpose his force between his own troops and those commanded by Johnson. Jackson in the North Fork would be able to concentrate his two forces if he had timely information as to Banks' movements.   Also the road in the North Fork Valley was better than in the South Fork Valley.   By blocking the roads which connected Frémont and Banks, Jackson secured his position and prevented Banks from getting information, as Ashby's cavalry stopped the Federal patrols moving up the Shenandoah Valley.

For ten days, Banks was ignorant of Jackson's movements. This uncertainty caused Banks to leave a quarter of his force to guard his communications back to Harper's Ferry.   By advancing towards Milroy at McDowell, Jackson gave Banks an opportunity to act on interior lines, but Jackson, calculating on Banks' deliberate movements, considered that he could do this with security.   He thus accurately estimated his opponent's capacity.

VII.—OFFENSIVE ACTION.

(a) Offensive action by giving the initiative adds to the confidence and efficiency of all ranks.   It demands, however, a superiority of some sort, in order to justify its assumption. There must be more men, larger resources, or the possibility of surprising or of enveloping the enemy, otherwise the offensive may have to be abandoned with the consequent loss of *morale*.

As long as the offensive can be maintained, there is always the possibility of decisive success, and there is the advantage of simplicity in the plan.

In this campaign the numbers and resources of the South would not justify their adoption of an offensive campaign.

At the outbreak of the war, the Federals were able to call up 180,000 men for service on land and at sea. Of these 16,000 were trained soldiers and 9,000 out of the total of 25,000 available for service at sea were trained sailors. Therefore, after the Battle of the First Bull Run on July 21st, 1861, the Confederates, though successful on the field, were unable to follow up the Federals and carry out an offensive campaign, as the commander did not think that their numbers were sufficient to deal with the two divisions that might be holding the Washington defences.

Actually the Confederate commander, Beauregard, did plan at this battle to carry out the offensive, and to cross the Bull Run River, and attack the left flank of the Federal position and cut off their forces from their base at Washington.

However, his orders miscarried, and the Federals' attack materialized before fresh orders could be carried out.

Beauregard's strength was insufficient for offensive action. His 2,500 sabres, 25,500 rifles and 29 guns were opposed by seven troops of cavalry, five infantry divisions, and 43 guns.

The possibilities for the offensive were all on the side of the Federals, both strategically and tactically. The total Confederate forces in the field were 32,000 as compared with the three invading Federal columns, which totalled 80,000.

The Confederates would only be able to take the offensive when chance offered of attacking isolated Federal troops, as their columns operating west of the Blue Ridge and west of Washington respectively were widely separated, whereas if a local offensive was to be undertaken in either area by the Confederates they could use the Manassas Railway running through the Bull Run Mountains at Thorofare Gap and over the Blue Ridge to Front Royal and Strasburg.

In this battle, however, the Federals had the superiority in numbers, which justified the assumption of the offensive.

However, by splitting up their forces and by sending their 2nd and 3rd Divisions south of Young's Branch, they lost their advantage. These two divisions were then charged and checked by Stuart's cavalry. Then they were held by the determined resistance of General Stonewall Jackson's Brigade at Henry House Hill.

His counter-attack, reinforced by the assault of the newly arrived brigade under Kirby Smith, enabled Beauregard to make a general offensive movement and to drive back the Federals from their position. Their effort to stand at Young's Branch was also rendered ineffective owing to the final attack of another Confederate brigade which had just reached the field.

The Federals' right flank was driven back and withdrew in disorder. Lack of discipline in the ranks and of organization in the staff prevented Johnston from continuing the offensive.

Had he been able to do so he could have captured the Arlington Heights dominating the Federal capital on July 22nd and 23rd, but the demoralization of the Confederates after their success made a co-ordinated plan of attack impossible.

(b) In the Battle of McDowell on May 8th, 1862, offensive tactics failed. In this case the Federal commander, Milroy, advancing from McDowell Village, crossed the Bull Pasture river by a bridge to attack the Confederates on Sitlington Hill.

The Federal numbers were not sufficient to warrant the assumption of the offensive. On both sides were approximately 6,000. The Federals were not adequately supported by artillery fire from Hull's Hill. After four hours, their attempts failed, and they retired.

(c) At the Battle of Winchester on May 25th, 1862, General Jackson had such a numerical superiority in sabres, guns, and rifles over the Federals that the assumption of the offensive was fully justified. He had sufficient numbers to enable him to carry out envelopment successfully.

His infantry were 16,000 strong as compared to 6,500 of the Federals, and he had three times as many guns. Though the Federals had a strong and well-chosen position on the hills south-west of Winchester, with one brigade on their left somewhat detached, being west of Abraham's Creek and a mile from their troops just west of the main Valley road, Jackson never wavered in his offensive actions during this battle.

When Ewell's advance was checked on his right, the attacks by his brigades on the other flank restored the situation.

Thus, when eleven Confederate regiments finally attacked the right flank of the Federal position covering Winchester, while other troops held them in front, the result was never in doubt. The Federals gave way and were driven back along the main road to Winchester, through this town and back towards the River Potomac, followed by all the available Confederate infantry.

The full results of this success could not be obtained, as it should have been by a continuance of the offensive. Ashby could collect only fifty men, as the rest had straggled, and Stuart, with 700 sabres, acting on the letter of his previous instructions, refused to pursue until he received definite orders.

Thus the opportunity of gaining a complete victory was allowed to slip.   Banks was able unmolested to cross the River Potomac on that night and next day.

Yet, although full tactical results were not obtained by this offensive operation, the effect was to save Richmond, as again for the third time President Lincoln interfered in McClellan's plans.   He ordered McDowell, who was on the point of marching to join the main Federal army, to send a brigade of cavalry and two divisions of infantry to the Valley to co-operate with Frémont in the support of Banks.

A reserve corps of 50,000 men was organized for the defence of the capital.   Thus troops were taken from the decisive place and McDowell's force was dispersed.

When Ewell's advance was checked on his right flank, the advance of the Louisiana, Taliaferro's, and Scott's Brigades was vigorously continued.   Their attack decided the battle.

The misconduct and mishandling of the Confederate cavalry alone saved Banks' troops from destruction.

(d) Jackson's offensive strategy in the Shenandoah Valley had most important results in shaking the *morale* of the Federal President and his commanders.   By rapidity of movement and by vigorous offensive tactics he gained important successes.

After the Battles of Kernstown, Front Royal, Winchester, and Port Republic, the President became apprehensive for the safety of his capital and changed his plans, preventing McDowell from joining McClellan.

In spite of the fact that the Federal numbers in the Valley were considerably more than Jackson could hope to get together, yet he was always on the offensive, and, owing to his insight, resource, and rapidity, was never in close contact with more than 10,000 of his enemy at any of his Valley battles.

(e) At the Battle of Port Republic on June 9th, Jackson's bold offensive action led to success.   The Federal position was a strong one east of Port Republic.   The left flank rested on an impenetrable wood, and the right flank extended to the South Fork river.

Eight battalions, supported by 16 guns and some cavalry, held this position, which dominated the ground over which the Confederates must advance.   Jackson nearly ruined his plan by taking the offensive with one brigade against Tyler's force of 2,500 men in a strong position without waiting for the remainder of his available force to come up and make a co-ordinated attack on the whole front.   He sent forward Winder's Brigade to attack the Federals' left flank.   This attack was repulsed. Jackson, however, maintained his objective and continued his offensive operations. He reinforced Winder with a regiment and some artillery, and he sent Taylor's Brigade to attack the Federals' left flank. Winder was ordered to make further attacks with his reinforcements and with his own brigade. Although these attacks were again unsuccessful, Taylor was able to develop his offensive operations successfully on the Federal left flank, supported by artillery fire. This continuous pressure against the Federals decided the battle and caused Tyler to recall his troops that were successfully pressing forward on the right of his position.

Jackson now sent Taliaferro with his brigade, in co-operation with Winder's Brigade, and some cavalry to continue the offensive operations and to pursue the Federals, who were driven several miles from the battlefield up the Luray-Front Royal road. Shields, too, fell back with the defeated Federal troops towards Luray and then marched to Manassas to join McDowell.

By the morning of June 14th, Frémont had joined Banks at Middletown.

CHAPTER IV.

COMMENTS ON BATTLES.

It has been said that if all the greatest soldiers that have ever lived could assemble in order to decide on the immutable laws in the art of war, there would be a wide divergence of opinion.

The uncertainties in war are so numerous that, although principles of war must be studied, it must be realized that in applying them it may be necessary to take risks and to modify them in accordance with the varying circumstances and with the limited knowledge of the whole facts of any situation. However, comments must be made, in order to stimulate thought, which alone, as has been aptly said, maketh a whole man. To be a whole man is not, as is meant in the quotation, possible, but it is possible by co-operation between a commander and his staff to arrive at a reasonable plan, which, if carried out wholeheartedly by all ranks, will be successful if *morale*, training, leadership, and armament are suited to the requirements of the appreciation of each situation.

A commander may be above the average in some points, but no human being is above it in all ways. It is important, therefore, that staff officers should be chosen to supplement and augment a commander's weak points, so that all work harmoniously to attain the result of the commander's final plan.

In the following comments, emphasis is placed on the facts, from which it may be possible to learn in order to prepare for future wars:—

Bull Run ... ... July 21st, 1861.
Kernstown ... ... March 23rd, 1862.
McDowell ... ... May 8th, 1862.
Winchester ... ... May 25th, 1862.
Cross Keys and Port Republic ... June 8th and 9th, 1862.

Battle of Bull Run, July 21st, 1861.

1. Beauregard, in taking up a position with his 12 brigades, 2,500 cavalry and 29 guns, adequately secured his front by

watching each of the six fords in his front between Union Mills and Stone Bridge.

But his reserve was not in a central position from which to reinforce rapidly any part of the front or take the offensive where opportunity occurred. The bulk of his reserve was behind his right flank.

The result was that his position was precarious when two Federal divisions crossed by the Red House and Sudley Fords to attack his left flank.

2. The value of offensive action was illustrated by the operations on the Confederates' left flank when the Federals' right advanced south-west down the Bull Run river and outflanked Beauregard.

Stuart's cavalry took the offensive and checked this advance, while Jackson's Brigade took up a position on Henry House Hill, and, by vigorous resistance, stopped their further progress.

Kirby Smith's Brigade detrained at Manassas Junction and took the offensive against the Federals' right flank. This caused them to withdraw to a position along Young's Branch, when again an attack on their southern flank made them retreat.

The final attacks by the Confederate cavalry with the offensive operations by two Confederate brigades from the river crossings at Union Mills and McLean's towards Centreville turned this retreat into a rout.

On the other hand, McDowell did not make use of his numerical superiority, nor use all his troops offensively either to press his original attack south of the river or to keep the Confederates engaged on their centre and right, so as to prevent them from reinforcing their left at the time when he had gained an initial advantage.

3. The value of training was exemplified by the fact that both sides after the victory became demoralized.

Had the Confederates been able to carry out an organized pursuit, a decisive victory might have been gained and the Federal capital might have been occupied by them. On both sides the training of the staff was defective.

Beauregard wished to take the offensive on his right flank, to cover the River Bull Run, and to advance on Centreville at the beginning of the battle.

Owing to mistiming, the offensive against his left flank materialized before his attack started, and he was then forced to conform to the movements of the Federals by reinforcing his left to meet this attack.

Lack of preparation and organization by the staff, added to

lack of discipline by the troops, prevented the Confederates from turning their success into a victory by a vigorous and sustained pursuit.

The want of combination in the Federals' actions and the delay in not starting the battle on July 19th or 20th before Beauregard had been reinforced, was due to their faulty staff work.

4. F.S.R., Vol. II, tell us that " detailed and timely information about the enemy and the theatre of operations is a necessary factor for success in war."

The Confederates were surprised by the Federals' attack on their left, as they had not used their cavalry to scout in this direction.   Johnston was able to move his force of 10,000 men to Bull Run battlefield away from the Valley unknown to Patterson, who, with 14,000 men, was operating there to prevent this co-operation.

This was possible owing to Patterson's lack of information as to Johnston's numbers and movements.

BATTLE OF KERNSTOWN, MARCH 23RD, 1862.

1. The value of a commander keeping in view the general objective of the campaign was exemplified by this battle.

In the vicinity of Kernstown Jackson had only three infantry brigades—that is, 3,400 infantry, 290 cavalry, and 27 guns, as compared with Shields' 7,000 rifles, 750 sabres, and 24 guns.

In spite of this inferiority in numbers, Jackson determined to make a diversion in order to detain the Federals in the Valley and to prevent further reinforcements being sent to McClellan.

The result of this battle, undertaken under sound strategical principles, was that, although it was a tactical reverse for Jackson, yet it made the Federal President apprehensive as to the safety of his capital, and in consequence he did not reinforce his main army at the decisive point in the Yorktown Peninsula.

2. Necessity for accurate information was brought out by the dangerous distribution of Jackson's force in his initial attack.   This was based on Ashby's information that there was only Shields' rearguard, about 3,000 strong, in his front.

Nor would Jackson probably have attacked so soon after his arrival at Kernstown on the 23rd at the end of a fourteen-mile march when, on the previous day, his troops had covered twenty-two miles.   Acting then on incorrect knowledge, he divided his forces.

He sent two-thirds of his infantry and one battery to a commanding position on a ridge west of Middle road in an endeavour to turn the Federals' right.   Had he been able to maintain the position occupied behind a stone wall on this ridge and to have covered a further advance from it against Kimball's right flank and rear, the operation might have been decisive.

As it was, he ran a considerable risk.   He brought from his reserve two battalions and four batteries to join the troops on the ridge, thus exposing the small remainder to the possibility of being defeated by superior forces and to the remainder of his brigade being then cut off from their line of retreat.

He increased the fatigue of his troops by a four-mile march over undulating wooded country for this enveloping movement, and left only 200 cavalry and one battalion to make a holding frontal attack and to guard his train on the Valley turnpike.

If either of his forces was attacked, there could be no active co-operation owing to the distance between the two bodies of troops.

3. The value of taking the initiative is shown by the fact that Kimball, seeing the danger to his right flank and rear, conformed to Jackson's operations and sent Tyler's Brigade to attack the Confederates on the ridge.

Another result of taking the initiative was that the Federal commander overestimated Jackson's numbers.

Had the Federals used their numerical superiority to counter-attack down the main road while containing Jackson's troops, the result might have been disastrous for the Confederates, with little loss to the Federals.

As it was, although the Confederates were forced to withdraw in front of Tyler's and Sullivan's Brigades on the ridge, yet they were not disorganized.   The Federals had 570 casualties without gaining any decisive result.

4. " Without pursuit there can be no complete victory." After this battle the Federal infantry were so disorganized that they could not pursue.   The Federal cavalry were unequal in training and *morale* to the Confederate horsemen, and, though superior in numbers to those under the command of Ashby, yet they were not able to harass the withdrawal.

Jackson was therefore able to march in his own time southwards to Newtown.

5. It should be noted that Garnett withdrew his brigade without orders and without having suffered any great loss, and while it would have been possible to get into communication with his commander.   Jackson maintained that his failure

was brought about by Garnett's retirement, but it is evident that the small Confederate force was incapable of defeating the larger numbers opposed to him.

6. Jackson's orders to Ashby to hold the Federals by demonstrations were inadequate. Ashby's small force of cavalry with a few infantry was incapable of carrying out the rôle allotted to it. To hold a force it is necessary to be able to attack it with sufficient vigour to keep it engaged. If the Federals had been more concentrated earlier in the engagement, it is possible that a counter-attack down the main road might have been disastrous to the Confederates, for it would have been possible to have held Jackson's flank attack while directing the main stroke against his reserves and transport.

BATTLE OF McDOWELL, MAY 8TH, 1862.

1. A position must be strategically important, otherwise there will be no need for an opponent to attack it. In this case, Jackson, in his advance on McDowell Village, occupied Sitlington's Hill.

From this position McDowell and the Federal camp could be commanded.

Jackson occupied this position with six battalions and had his cavalry in the defile on the west of Hull's Hill. When the Federals did attack they were not supported effectively by artillery fire, and, though they combined a flank attack by 1,500 men with a frontal attack from two battalions, they were driven back.

2. Although the Confederates were successful in repulsing the Federals' attacks, yet they were not able to gain a complete victory, as their pursuit of the infantry was delayed by forest fires, and the country was not suitable for the action of cavalry.

During the night the Federals were able to reach Franklin.

3. The Federal commander did not carry out the Principle of Concentration of Force. He employed only 2,500 men out of the 6,000 men who were available. Consequently his troops were driven back after four hours' fighting, and it became necessary to withdraw after dark towards Franklin, as McDowell Village was untenable with the Confederates on the dominating position of Sitlington's Hill.

BATTLE OF WINCHESTER, MAY 25TH, 1862.

1. The Federal commander was ignorant of the movements in his front because he did not give his cavalry clear and

definite orders to carry out specific missions.   His detached
force at Front Royal had no cavalry at all, and it was completely surprised by Jackson's attack.

When he heard of the result of Kenly's action at this place,
he had great difficulty in deciding on his course of action
owing to his ignorance of the actual situation.

It was possible to wait for reinforcements from the 17,500
men under Frémont at Franklin, to attack at once towards
Front Royal, to withdraw in an easterly direction, or to
advance towards the River Potomac.

He withdrew along the road to Winchester, where his force,
6,500 strong, was confronted by 16,000 Confederates.

2. The value of a strong position, unless it is occupied
with a view to active defence, is shown by the one taken up
by the Federals covering Winchester on the south and south-
west.

This position was protected in front by Abraham's Creek.

Jackson's advanced guard contained the troops south-west
of Winchester, while Ewell's divisions attacked those south of
this town on the north bank of the creek, and Campbell's,
Taliaferro's and Taylor's Brigades on the west of the position
turned Banks' right flank.

The result of these active operations was to force the
Federals to give way on their whole front, although at first
they had successfully resisted Ewell's attacks.   When the
Federals' right flank was finally turned by the enveloping
movement of Taylor's Brigade, Jackson took the offensive
on his whole front, and Banks' force retired.

3. Had the Confederate cavalry carried out their rôle of
acting vigorously during the final phase of these operations,
Burnside's routed army would have been completely defeated.
Ashby's cavalry, however, scattered to pillage, and Stuart
waited for definite orders from Ewell before following up the
retreating Federals.

When Stuart did receive his orders he pursued the Federals
up to Martinsburg.

4. The immediate result of Jackson's offensive operations
against Banks at Front Royal and Winchester, followed by
his quick pursuit to Harper's Ferry, was that the Federals
under Banks had lost a third of their effective strength in
casualties, 3,000 prisoners, two guns and much stores had
been captured, and they had been driven over the River
Potomac.

The effect of these disasters on Lincoln was to cause him
to order McDowell to send 20,000 men to the Shenandoah

Valley to operate with Frémont, who was to advance from Franklin to Harrisonburg.

McDowell's co-operation with McClellan in the Yorktown Peninsula was stopped.

BATTLE OF CROSS KEYS, JUNE 8TH, 1862.

BATTLE OF PORT REPUBLIC, JUNE 9TH, 1862.

1. The necessity for space in which to make full use of mobility was brought out in these battles. Jackson, with 13,000 men was operating on interior lines, and, though numerically inferior to Frémont and Shields if they combined, had to make full use of his mobility to defeat them in detail.

As the distance between the two battlefields was only two and a half miles, Jackson could not disregard one opponent while he attacked the other.

On June 9th, Jackson had to leave Trimble's and Patton's Brigades to contain Frémont at Cross Keys while he crossed the river and defeated Shields' advancing troops—namely, Tyler's and Carroll's Brigades—before they could be supported.

2. The failure of the Federals' attack, in spite of their superiority of numbers, at Cross Keys was due to the fact that Frémont did not make concerted, simultaneous attacks. He sent one division first to attack Ewell's right flank. This division was outflanked and driven back with loss before his attack against Ewell's left materialized.

The lack of co-operation between Frémont and Shields was most marked, as Shields made no effort on June 8th to create a diversion in favour of Frémont by attacking.

Similarly, on the 9th, when Jackson recalled the three brigades left at Cross Keys to his battle at Port Republic, Frémont had an opportunity of co-operating with Shields by following them up vigorously and preventing them from being used. Instead Frémont moved very slowly and only occupied the hills west of the South Fork after Tyler had been driven back.

3. Jackson's first attack failed at Port Republic on June 9th, as it was made with insufficient numbers. He sent Winder's Brigade ahead of Taylor's Brigade, which had been delayed in crossing the river. Later he was successful when he attacked with three brigades against Tyler's forward force of 2,500 men.

4. The value of flank attacks when successful was shown by the fact that, though Tyler was able to drive back Winder's Brigade operating on his right flank, yet when the pressure of Taylor's Brigade on his left became pronounced he withdrew his victorious troops.

Jackson was then able to make a general advance with the additional help of two of the brigades withdrawn from Frémont's front, and drove the Federals north along the Luray road.

5. The value of Jackson's strategic counter-offensive was again considerable. Shields was detained at Luray, another division was kept at Front Royal, McDowell's co-operation with McClellan was again stopped. Jackson, who had marched to Brown's Gap, was now free to join Lee in the main battle taking place east of Richmond.

Allan, in " Jackson's Valley Campaign," reviews the operations of the three months preceding the Battles of Cross Keys and Port Republic as follows: —

" Jackson, with 4,600 men, fell back from Winchester before Banks' 30,000, but appearing unexpectedly at Kernstown hurls his little army against part of Banks' army. He is mistaken as to the number of the enemy, and suffers a severe repulse; but he causes the recall of all Banks' force and the detachment of McDowell from McClellan. Falling back before his pursuers, he retires to Elk Run Valley, where he leaves Ewell to contain Banks, while he himself joins Ed Johnson near Staunton. He fights Milroy at McDowell, and drives him back on General Frémont. Jackson then countermarches, and with Ewell unexpectedly appears at Front Royal, crushes a Federal detachment there, and two days after defeats Banks at Winchester, driving him over the River Potomac.

" McDowell is again withdrawn from McClellan and the President gathers 60,000 men against Jackson's 16,000; but by rapidity he eludes his pursuers, and, retiring up the Valley, takes up a position near Port Republic, where he defeats Frémont at Cross Keys and Shields at Port Republic."

S. C. Kellogg gives this tribute to General Jackson in his " Shenandoah Valley ": " The student must be impressed with the strategical eminence of Stonewall Jackson, as compared with the lack of capacity on the part of his opponents."

INDEX

67

SHENANDOAH VALLEY 1862

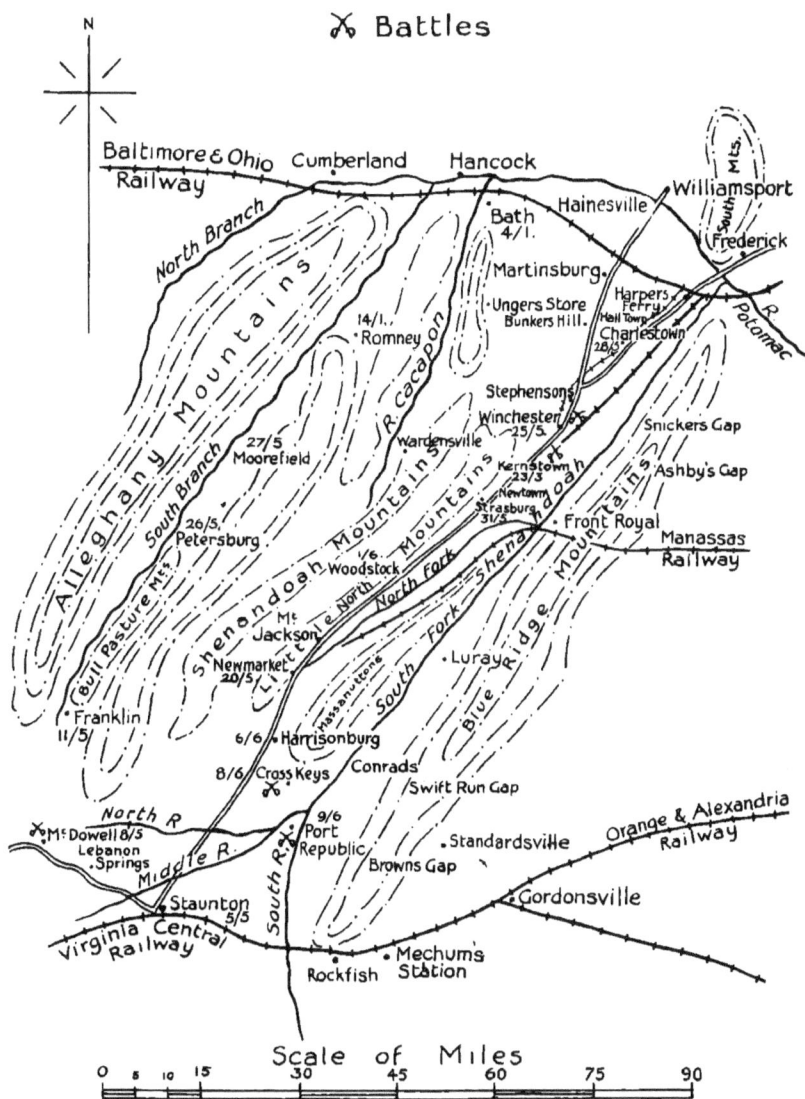

�֍ Battles

N

Baltimore & Ohio Railway
Cumberland
Hancock
Bath 4/1.
Hainesville
Williamsport
South Mts.
Frederick
North Branch
Martinsburg.
Ungers Store
Bunkers Hill.
Harpers Ferry
Hall Town
Charlestown 28/5
Potomac R.
14/1. Romney
R. cacapon
Stephensons
Winchester 25/5
Snickers Gap
Alleghany Mountains
27/5 Moorefield
Wardensville
Kernstown 23/3
Newtown
Strasburg 1/6 31/5
Ashby's Gap
South Branch
26/5 Petersburg.
Bull Pasture Mts.
Shenandoah Mountains
Little North
North Fork
Woodstock
Mt Jackson
South Fork Shenandoah
Front Royal
Manassas Railway
Blue Ridge Mountains
Newmarket 20/5
Massanuttone
South Fork
Luray
Franklin 11/5/
6/6 Harrisonburg
8/6 Cross Keys
Conrads
Swift Run Gap
✗McDowell 8/5
Lebanon Springs
North R
9/6 Port Republic
Standardsville
Browns Gap
Orange & Alexandria Railway
Middle R.
Staunton 5/5
South R.
Gordonsville
Virginia Central Railway
Rockfish
Mechum's Station

Scale of Miles

0 5 10 15 30 45 60 75 90

G.E.P.

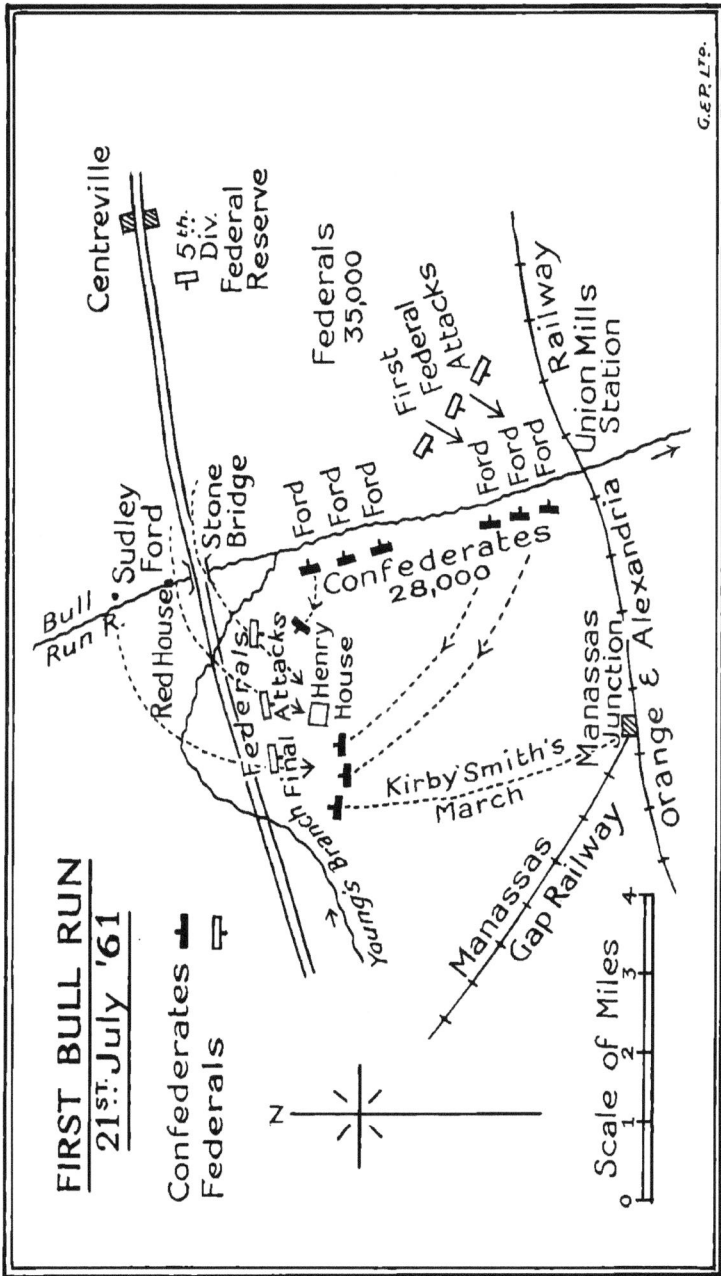

FIRST BULL RUN
21ST July '61

Confederates ━┿
Federals ┏┓

Centreville

5th. Div.
Federal
Reserve

Federals
35,000

First
Federal
Attacks

Railway

Union Mills
Station

Sudley Ford

Stone
Bridge

Red House

Ford
Ford
Ford

Ford
Ford
Ford

Bull
Run R.

Federals
Final Attacks

Henry
House

Confederates
28,000

Kirby Smith's
March

Manassas
Junction

Orange & Alexandria

Young's Branch

Manassas
Gap Railway

Scale of Miles
0   1   2   3   4

N

G. & P. LTD.

KERNSTOWN
23rd March. 1862

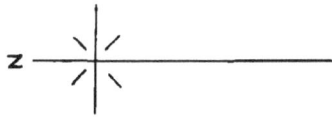

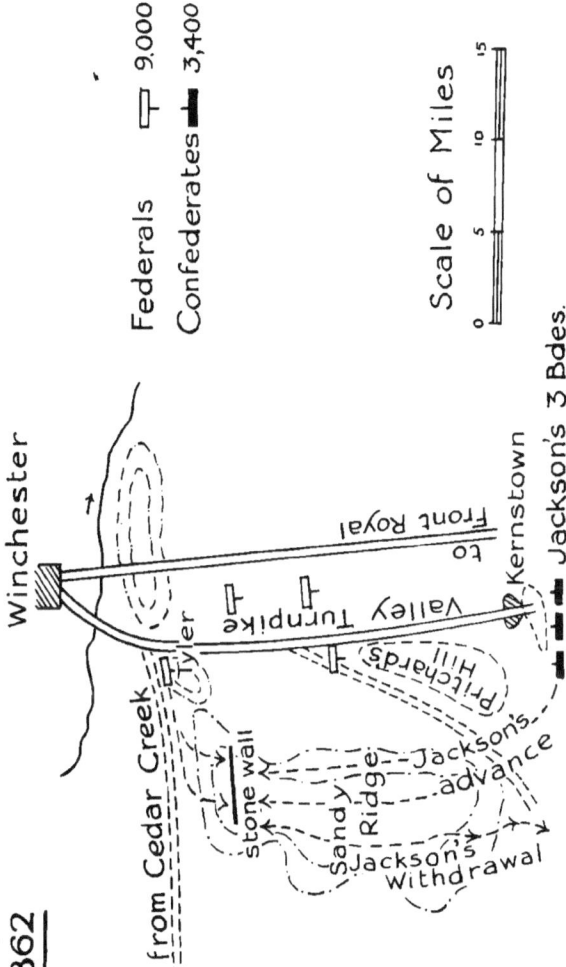

Winchester

from Cedar Creek

stone wall

Sandy Ridge

Tyler

Valley Turnpike

Pritchards Hill

to Front Royal

Kernstown

Jackson's advance

Jackson's withdrawal

Jackson's 3 Bdes.

Federals 9.000
Confederates 3,400

Scale of Miles
0   5   10   15

G.E.P. LTP

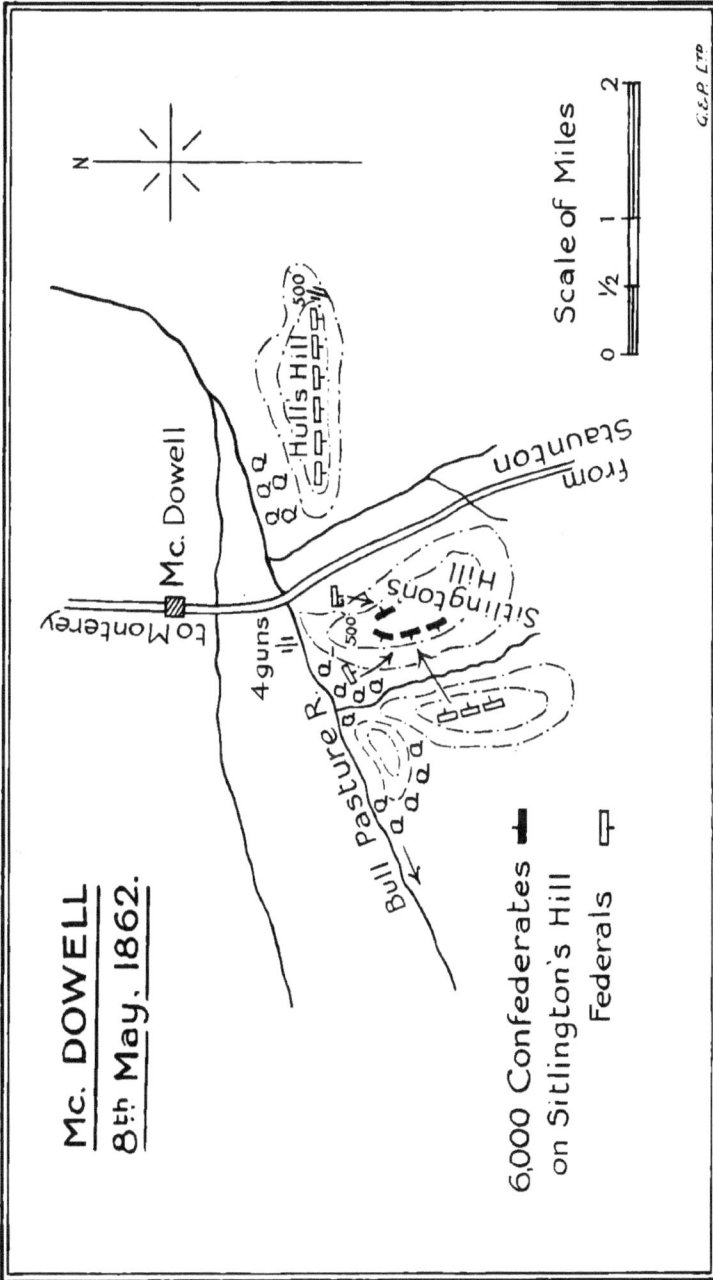

Mc. DOWELL
8th May. 1862.

to Monterey

Mc. Dowell

Hulls Hill
500

from Staunton

Sitlington's Hill

4 guns

500

Bull Pasture R.

N

Scale of Miles

0   ½   1   2

G.E.P. LTD

6,000 Confederates
on Sitlington's Hill

Federals

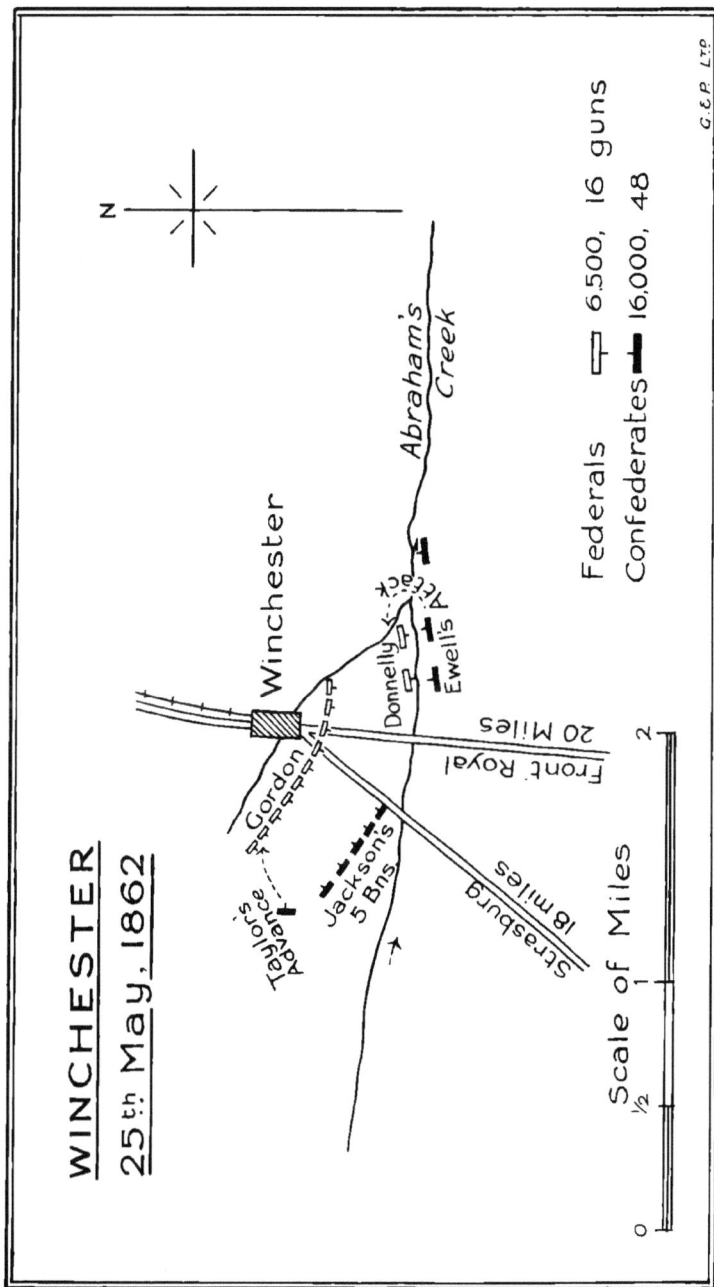

WINCHESTER
25th May, 1862

N

Winchester

Abraham's Creek

Donnelly's Attack

Ewell's A.

Gordon

Taylor's Advance

Jackson's 5 Bns.

Front Royal 20 Miles

Strasburg 18 miles

Federals ▭ 6,500, 16 guns

Confederates ▬ 16,000, 48

Scale of Miles

0   ½   1   2

G.&.P. LTD.

7

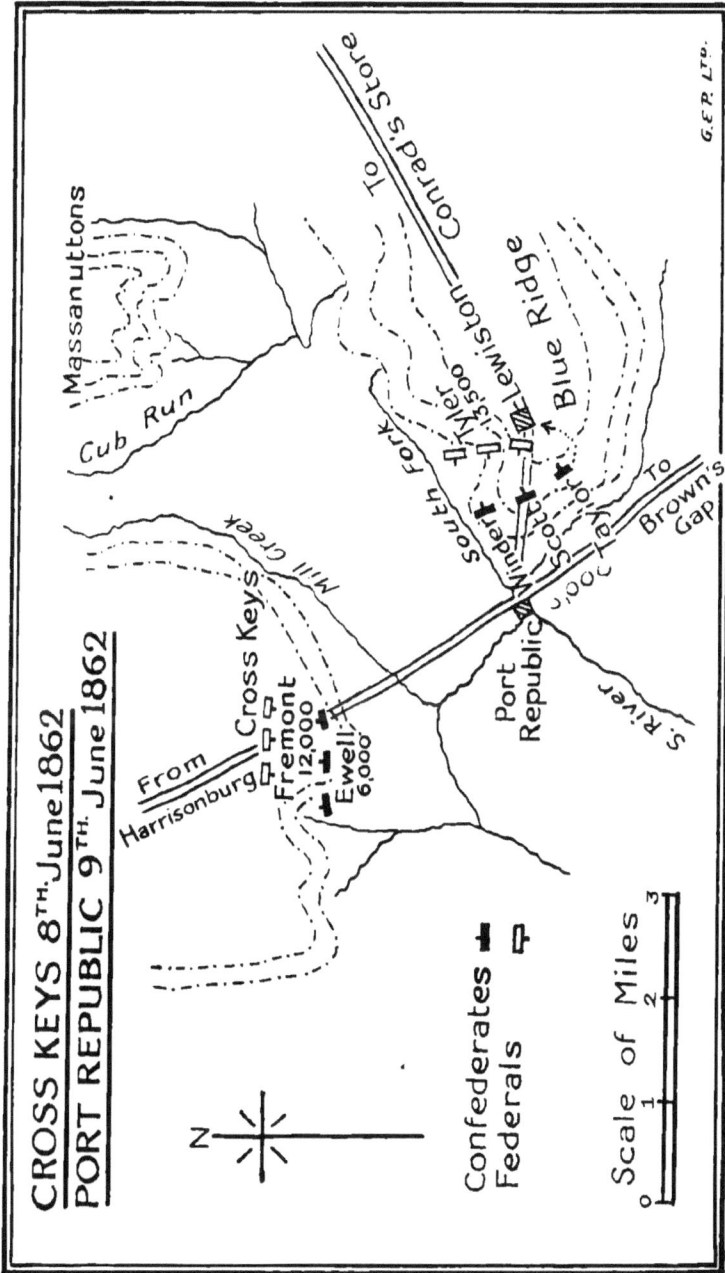

CROSS KEYS 8TH.June 1862
PORT REPUBLIC 9TH. June 1862

Massanuttons

Cub Run

To Conrad's Store

Tyler
15,000
Lewiston
Blue Ridge

South Fork
Winder
Scott
S. Fork

Mill Creek

Cross Keys

From Harrisonburg

Fremont
12,000

Ewell
6,000

Port Republic

To Brown's Gap

S. River

N

Confederates
Federals

Scale of Miles
0 1 2 3

G.E.P. LTD.